A (

my luggage

A camera in
my luggage

Nick Smith

Bay Books
2020

A Camera in My Luggage

First published in Great Britain in 2020
Bay Books, 1 Cae Banc, Sketty, Swansea, SA2 9DN

Copyright © 2020 Nick Smith

Nick Smith has asserted his moral rights

A CIP catalogue record of this book is available from the British Library

ISBN 978-0-9571104-2-7

Typeset in Times New Roman by the author
Cover design: Simon Williams
Text ornaments: Jenny Balfour Paul
Copy editor: Nicky Watts

Printed by BookPrintingUK

Printed on FSC accredited paper sourced from renewable, responsible sources.

First edition, first impression

For my daughter, Tegan

Also by Nick Smith

Travels in the World of Books
Travels in Search of a Photograph
Did You Hear the One About…

As editor
The Strange Case of Mr Pelham
Questions & Answers

As contributor
The DK Book of Exploration

Contents

Preface

Read the first few lines of *A Camera in My Luggage* and you will have little choice but to continue to the last page, for Nick Smith is a man of wide and varied literary and photography accomplishments and, as one would expect, he achieves much with *A Camera in My Luggage*.

Through the ingenious device of having no images whatsoever in his book, he challenges our preconceived ideas as to the motivation behind making images, while brazenly raising questions as to why photographers take up the camera in the first place. This is a book for those who, like me may well have taken a million photographs, as much as it is for those who have taken none.

There is rarely a page without a juicy anecdote or a delightful passage of self-effacement and side-splitting humour. There is something of a top comedian often emerging from within these pages, and a chronicler with an enviable memory for absolutely every event and incident that he has either endured or revelled in.

A Camera in My Luggage explodes photography into a zillion pieces and binds the craft and the processes back together in superb bite-size pieces that will, no doubt, forever endure in the memory of the reader.

Charlie Waite,
Eccliffe Mill, Dorset

Preamble

Let me see if I've got this right, said Hartley as we idled away a juicy London sunset, drinking beer on the fag-butt littered pavement outside Soho's famous *Dog & Duck.* "You're writing a book about photography, and there's not going to be any photographs in it..."

"Not one," I replied, pleased with myself and hoping for approval of the concept from my friend, a polar adventure photographer of international renown.

"It sounds like a bit of a daft idea, if you ask me," snorted Hartley as he returned to the business of polishing off the remains of his pint that was by now little more than a brown stain on the bottom of his glass.

As he sauntered off to the bar to fetch refills, I thought about his comment that was still ringing in the ears: *It sounds like a bit of a daft idea.* And I suppose, on the surface, it might be. But, I reasoned, there are plenty of books on classical music without any accompanying audio, and there are hardly any recipe books that come fresh from the printer with a lasagne stuck on the cover. Given that today's newspapers could hardly be any worse if they were to be printed without photographs, it seemed to me that we really don't need to be quite so literally minded that a book about photography should contain photographs. The more I thought about the idea, the more convinced I became that I had a reasonable point, and then someone tolled a bell and it was time to go home.

"Yer daft," reiterated Hartley, as he disappeared into Tottenham Court Road tube station. "A book about photography has got to have photos in it. Everyone knows that. Mark my words. Yer a damned fool."

A few months later Hartley and I were loafing at the *Dog & Duck* once again, only this time sitting beside an autumn log fire, going over the same old ground. "How's yer mad non-photographic photography book coming along then?" he asked, his voice teetering somewhere between a cheery laugh and a sarcastic snarl. "You're going to tell me it's got no words in it now, are you?"

I kept my thoughts private, partially because I know when I'm being ragged, but also because as much as I enjoy boozy arguments, Hartley was beginning to have a clear view of the finishing line. Having satisfied himself that the game was in the bag, he hammered his victory home: "I mean, what's the *point*?"

The point, I nearly countered, was that we're so used to looking at photographs that we tend to forget to think about them. And sometimes the best way to think about something is to remove yourself from its presence, to step back and reflect from a distance. Surely the best cricket matches are won in the dead of the night, when the skipper rehearses his bowling changes, analyses the meteorological and terrestrial conditions, bluffs and double bluffs the opposition. Certainly the most sublime music is written in the composer's head long before he sits at the piano and dictates the notes to himself. I toyed with the idea of explaining all this to the increasingly sceptical Hartley, but relegated these notions to being ones you keep to yourself. It's sometimes better that way.

But every now and then the writer finds that he can't keep his ideas to himself, even if they are on the subject of photography, and even if they do sound a bit daft to others. "I'll tell you what," I eventually said to my baffled friend, "if you think it's such a colossally bad idea, why does the editor of *Outdoor Photography* magazine keep commissioning my column month in month out?"

"Now that beats me," says Hartley, "he's normally such a reasonable bloke." And with that the subject was closed, never to be raised again. *NS*

*"A photograph is usually
looked at: seldom looked into"*

Ansel Adams (1902-84)

1

Photography at the
Friday Philosophy Club

Have you ever wondered why we take photographs?
We'll all say at one time or another that, on the surface
at least, our purpose is to capture a moment or a feeling.
But there's more to it than that. Or is there?

Cycling along the Brighton seafront one sunshine, ice cream, helter-skelter Whitsun afternoon, my daughter asked me an extremely interesting question. She wanted to know how I can write endlessly on photography and yet never run out of things to say about it. As a writer who has interviewed several hundreds of photographers about what they do and why they never run out of things to shoot, I thought my daughter's question fair, and set to ordering my thoughts on the seemingly limitless subject of photography, why we do it and what it's for.

No-one really knows why they take photographs. Take my word for it. In all the interviews I've conducted I've rarely received any response more evolved than it being something to do with 'capturing a moment or an emotion'. There's nothing wrong with this, and while I can broadly speaking accept that there might be a purity of motive that's both hard to pin down and yet widespread enough to be a consensus, this approach doesn't seem to be quite enough. Not for me, in any case.

In linguistics there's a term for a combination of words that occur more frequently than would be expected by chance, and it's one we use every day. An idiom can, of course, become a cliché when over-used, and I think we can all agree that when footballers routinely describe themselves as being either 'over the moon' or 'sick as a parrot', we're not delving very deep into their psyche. An overlooked aspect of the interviewer's job is the quest to uncover what lies beneath these phrases. As unfair as it might sound, I often start my investigations into a photographer's outlook on the process with: "I know we're all trying to capture a moment or an emotion. But what I'm interested in is why."

Ansel Adams once said that photographs are often looked at, but seldom looked into. I'm tempted to continue that train of thought by stating that when we do look into them, a conclusion we often reach is that words aren't always a useful tool for describing what's there. In a different artistic orbit, this is a sentiment shared by Thelonious Monk who said that writing about music is like dancing about architecture. While these are finely tuned words, they also seem to say it's all right for us to give up our pursuit of significant meaning simply because it's difficult. It gets even worse when we go beyond why we do it and start to think about what it all means. Cleverly ducking the issue, Bob Dylan, when asked what one of his songs was about, replied that it was 'about three minutes long'. When asked what his fabulously opaque classic song *American Pie* meant, Don McLean revealed a more translucent side to his character, replying that it meant he'd never have to work again.

It's much easier to tackle these questions when you're young. As a corduroy-jacketed comprehensive school sixth former, I used to pass those dark and rainy winter Friday lunchtimes at Philosophy Club, in which we'd debate topics ranging from nuclear disarmament to the nature of free will. It was all fascinating and exciting, even more so looking back, peering at the past over a pile of everyday paperwork that seems so hostile compared with the act of enthusiastic and naïve debate. The topic I always enjoyed most – which probably means the one I was most opinionated on – was the nature, purpose and value of art. "What is art?" we used to ask the world in general, before reminding ourselves that the first rule of Philosophy Club was that you don't make intellectually vain statements that cast no light on anything.

Talking of art, as photographers we all seem to be divided over whether we regard what we do is an art or a craft. While there is a defined body among us that is suspicious of fine art photography – I was once told by a landscaper that it was just an excuse to add a few zeroes to the price of a print – none of us seems to mind being called an artisan, as this somehow dignifies the level of expertise and experience associated with a craft.

Dylan Thomas split the difference when he referred to his poetry as a 'Craft or Sullen Art', irritatingly throwing bias on the latter through the use of an intensifying adjective. But then again, the Welshman was more concerned with what his poems sounded like than what they meant. In a similar vein, we have photographers who are more concerned with what their work looks like than what it means, while there are plenty who will happily tell you that what their work means is more important than what it looks like. Then there are those who will tell you that the two ideas can't be separated. And there are also those who will cheerfully admit that the distinction has never entered their mind.

I somewhat like the idea that while we have an innate understanding of the purpose of what we are trying to do, we struggle to articulate it. I like the idea that some photographers choose to express themselves in a non-verbal medium precisely because it is difficult to translate into words what we feel about what we see.

On the other hand, I'm attracted to the approach of photographers who give their works abstract and challenging titles, present them alongside poems by their own or another's hand, or feel the need to verbally dissect their intentions. I also think that there are times – especially when I'm faced with those annoying 'artist's statements' you see at degree shows – when we should just shut up and get on with it, leaving the big questions to daughters on bicycles.

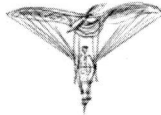

2

Playing the long
game in Spain

*After decades of roaming the globe in pursuit of the craft
of travel photography, I'm starting to think the cardinal
lesson to be learned is that we acquire more insight into
the art of image making by staying in one place...*

As a photojournalist one of the things I look forward to
most is my monthly interviews with photographers. It
doesn't matter if they're just starting out or diehard
veterans, amateur or professional, I generally walk away
from these conversations with a heightened understanding
of what it means to be someone who takes photographs.
These dialogues always feed fresh ideas into my own
photography. It's a great way to learn.

After more than a decade of speaking with the brightest
and the best, there isn't much that surprises me about the
process though. And yet, recently I was taken flat aback
by one of my interviewees who, provoked by the spirit of

enquiry, turned the tables in a rather unorthodox manner by asking me about my work. "How do you describe yourself as a photographer?" he enquired, casually pinching my best probing device. "Well..." quoth I, "I'm sometimes called a travel photographer. But I'm reluctant to use that tag, because I don't know what it means." After a moment's thought, having decided that it was unfair to describe myself in terms of what I am not, I told him I'm a 'spot' photographer.

My answer falling dully on stony ground, I further thought it reasonable to explain why I should choose such an archaic descriptor. Despite being a vague-sounding expression, 'spot' (short for 'on the spot') photography has – or at least used to have – a specific meaning in that it describes reacting spontaneously to a scene, without an established plan. *Reportage,* if you like. I then suggested that this is necessarily a staple of travel photography, the pursuit of which apparently random enterprise has taken me all over the globe for decades. I've taken a camera in my luggage with me to more countries than most people can name. I've reported from six continents, while I'm saving Australasia for when there's sufficient time to follow an entire Ashes series.

Clearly feeling sorry for me, my inquisitor wondered if I ever became frustrated with shooting "different subjects all the time, never knowing what they're going to be, or what the conditions will be like." To which I answered in the affirmative, offering the defence that what I do is a job like any other, and that sometimes 'big picture' concerns – such as making a living – trumps the aesthetic agenda. As with any job, there are downsides: mine being airports, mosquitoes and an empty wallet.

"But the upside," I countered, "is that I can keep the home-fires of my 'long project' burning without feeling any pressure to see it in print." I realise now that I sounded as unconvincing as a musician who's not been heard of for some time talking about a 'background solo project', or even worse, an actor 'spending more time with the family'.

About a quarter of a century ago I was given a piece of advice by a very senior photographer, who told me that if I ever wanted to get good at this photography lark, or even stand a chance of marginally improving, the first and by far the best course of action was to pick a subject, stick to it and photograph it frequently over a long period of time. "You must keep returning to the scene of the crime," he said. "I don't care what your subject is, the trick is to just keep plugging away."

Given that my professional work hardly ever takes me to the same place twice, this seemed to present a conflict of possibilities. "You've got to get into the *habit* of taking really good shots. The habit must become reflex, and that reflex needs to be reliable in all circumstances," he continued. "Once you've learned something about how to photograph the robins in your garden or sunsets by the local lake, you can then transfer all this knowledge and experience into the reality of taking well-executed one-off compositions when it counts."

Shortly after this discussion I found myself high in the Alpujarras mountain region in southern Spain, where something quite peculiar happened. As I hiked up the mighty Mulhacén, I felt a strange compulsion to take an image of it with my camera. This wasn't the feeling I was accustomed to: that of grabbing an attractive shot that might look good in a magazine. This was more akin to a 'calling'. It sounds a bit pretentious I know, but I was suddenly possessed of the idea that I needed to create an image of the mountain that said something about it in the way that Augustus John's glorious painting of that very same scene did. The idea came, of course, from the cover of my copy of Gerald Brenan's lovely memoir of his peregrinations in the region – *South from Granada* – that I was carrying in my backpack. And so I decided that my journey would start from the same vantage point as John's painting. To find it required days of scouring and scouting the mountains, looking deeply into the landscape, getting to know the birds and butterflies, the scents and the sounds of its wildflowers, waterfalls and rivers.

I know that this is usually when people say that they caught the bug. But I didn't catch the bug. I was bitten by it, and bitten hard, its slow sweet poison creating an addiction that is with me still as I return to southern Spain several times a year, every year, to try to make sense of it all. Over time, the obsession has spread out east to the Mediterranean, up north to the Pyrenees, to the great cities and Spain's wild open interior. With each trip I try to add one, maybe two, images to a portfolio that progresses at glacial pace, that no-one has ever set eyes on.

"Oh, I see," said my interviewee-turned-interviewer on the other end of the line. "That sounds like a nice way of doing things, don't you think?"

I do indeed.

3

'Tis the season
to take photos?

*When it comes to Christmas, unless we are very lucky,
we inevitably experience a sense of dread. All that time
wasted indoors watching telly and eating seems a bit
gratuitous. So, when do we get to take our festive photos?*

People who don't revel in Christmas are traditionally
thought of as killjoy Grinches who should lighten up a
little and learn to love the Yuletide. But increasingly,
I find this more and more difficult to do. It's not that I
don't like the Nativity, the family get-togethers, or even
those boring round-robin letters from old school friends
you never see. It's just that as a holiday feast, it seems to
take so much time out of my life. Let's forget for a
moment that we've had to save days of our holiday
entitlement for such disproportionate reward. Let's also
forget the hammering our bank balances receive in
exchange for a wanton profligacy that is so difficult to

avoid. What really bothers me is that this is the time of year when I am boringly and terminally housebound. It's not that I'm against endless reruns of *Morecambe and Wise* or *Porridge*. Neither am I against Her Majesty the Queen, God bless her, wishing me all the jolly best on this day of days. I also wholeheartedly approve of those glorious repeats of *Top of the Pops* from the 1970s. But there really comes a point, once the turkey has been dispatched and the Christmas pudding has been consumed in fire, when I think it's high time we say to ourselves: "Enough's enough. Let's do something different. Let's stop sitting on our backsides playing boring board games and making annual phone calls to relatives we hardly know. Let's do something constructive instead."

Every year, in early December I start to get very excited because I convince myself that this will be the year St Nicholas brings me a new camera of great swank. By the time Christmas Eve arrives I can barely contain my excitement. As the festive dawn breaks, I bound downstairs with boyish enthusiasm to examine the presents stashed under the Christmas tree, certain that there will be a mound of lenses and laptops just waiting for me to open. My disappointment is, of course, something I have learnt to live with. Nobody, it seems, ever presents you with a gift that you might actually want. And so, with as much grace as I can muster, I put on my Christmas jumper and *Home Alone* socks, accepting that there is no such thing as a photographer's Christmas.

Why should there be? None of my musician friends ever gets a new Fender Stratocaster, while no cricketers of my acquaintance stroll up to the pub for our pre-Christmas luncheon pint brandishing a new Gray-Nicolls willow. But we all have a good laugh at each other's jumpers. And that's the way it should be. Now, let's assume that a Christmas miracle has happened, and that some batty old aunt has somehow managed to read your mind and has sent you one of those fantastic, glitzy, top-of-the-range compact cameras by Leica. You know the ones I mean: the sort of instrument that you've always wanted but could never quite justify the expense of when there is so much more quotidian gear that needs to be replaced, repaired or serviced. With trembling hands, you unwrap your present, gleefully noticing that Santa has done the decent thing by charging the batteries and popping a flashcard into the instrument's inner workings.

Like a kid with a new bike, all you want to do is get outside, impress your friends and have some fun. But of course, that's nigh-on impossible because this is the one day of the year when everybody decides that they're going to roast a turkey that is, with agricultural and culinary irony, the size of a sheep. You're hassled into coming back from the pub by 1 o'clock, by which time the festive fowl is barely dead, let alone cooked. By the time it's been carved and put on the table, the outside world is dark, and the Three Wise Men are on their way back to Persia, Egypt and India.

And so you watch *Strictly Come Dancing* in a house full of snoring relatives wondering why you never got to shoot a single frame that day. But that's okay, because as John Lennon said with lyrical sagacity that never fails to astound me: '... this is Christmas.' Had Lennon really been in the mood to blow our minds he might have taken it upon himself to remind us that the following day is the Feast of St Stephen, more commonly known as Boxing Day, when everything repeats itself. The only difference I can discern is that everyone is so hung over nobody minds if you disappear in the car for a couple of hours to take a few surreptitious photos.

But of course, the camera I've been describing doesn't really exist. Well, it does in a literal sense: but it doesn't exist in my world, because neither does the above-mentioned philanthropic batty old aunt. And so another glorious Christmas rolls by, inevitably the same as the last and identical to the next. But there's nothing particularly wrong with that either, and we should be sleepily content that our trusty old workhorse cameras have spent a day or two abandoned in the gadget bag.

Despite everyone now probably thinking that when it comes to this Christmas malarkey I'm little more evolved festively than Ebenezer Scrooge, I confess to having a soft spot for Noel-tide and its rituals of indulgence and indolence. It's just that a big part of me would rather be celebrating outdoors among the holly and the ivy.

4

The day the
earth stood still

*Could there ever be a day in your photographic life when
there was literally nothing to photograph? Impossible,
you may think. And yet, if such a terrible day really did
exist, what on earth would we do with our time?*

A journalist friend of mine, who is also a magazine
photographer, recently returned from one of those so-
called 'press trips' and was full of woe. For those of you
not entirely sure what a press trip is, it can be summarised
as follows. From time to time a tourism board, hotel
chain, airline or travel agent will send out an invitation
offering the chance to sample the delights of their product
– all expenses paid, of course – in exchange for your
guarantee that you will then write an article about said
experience in a national magazine or newspaper, which is
then decorated with your photographs and that all-
important internet link to the host's website. It's a form

of, if not bribery and corruption, then at least moral pressure on the freelancer to take a punt on whether the trip will generate sufficient publishable material to warrant the time and effort of travelling.

Most journalists are happy to take this bet because it's a pretty good one: the chances are that if you have been commissioned by a travel magazine to come up with a feature on, say, a luxury break in Barbados, and this is what actually happens, and the article eventually appears, then all honours are even and everyone is happy. As I say, it's not quite a Faustian pact, but it has the potential to create embarrassment, especially if, prior to going, you've uttered the phrase 'It should be all right', and you find out upon your return that it wasn't. This is exactly the position my friend found herself in as we sat in the *Dog & Duck* wondering what on earth she had let herself in for.

The critical aspect of her concern, which was rapidly becoming a downward spiral of despair, was that there had been nothing to photograph on the trip. This left her feeling that, while the piper had been generously paid, there wasn't much in the repertoire of tunes to be called. "You see," she said, "my big problem was that whenever we arrived somewhere interesting, it was at the wrong time of the day. And whenever it was the right time of day, we were inevitably crammed into a minibus chasing our tail because of itinerary slippage."

Itinerary slippage is one of the worst things that can happen to a photographer while on a press trip. This is because in order to get back on schedule, the organiser will brutally compress the remainder of the day's programme in order to reach journey's end on time. This is because, while everything else can wait, dinner can't, and the driver will be, under pain of death, ordered to get the delegation to the restaurant on time. Pity the poor togger, as we photographers sometimes call ourselves, left with nothing but the gloomy conclusion that even if there had been anything worthwhile to point the lens at, and even if the itinerary had taken into account the best time of day on which to point it at, then there would simply and inevitably be no time to do so.

Being of a helpful disposition, I gently asked my friend what was on her camera's data card. "Nothing," she moaned: "my picture editor is going to kill me."

I tried to rationalise her position by offering my opinion that while this was probably a dark view of the likely outcome, she was also certainly in something of a pickle. But this was as nothing, I assured her, compared with the day I had on a recent trip to the Galápagos Islands when there *really was nothing* to photograph. Despite my being of neither practical use nor comfort to her, my friend's curiosity was roused to the point where she seemed to temporarily forget her sorrows in favour of attending to mine. "Really?" she asked with the air of someone who'd not quite finished talking about herself.

In a curious variation on the 'marooned on a desert island' motif, I was stuck on a small cruise ship in the Pacific, off the coast of Ecuador. For reasons too boring to explain, we were not only unable to make landfall that day, but we weren't even within sight of land. There were no birds dropping in to scavenge from the galley and neither was there any mammalian marine life tootling by. I know that all the books of photographic wisdom will tell you that there is never, under any circumstances, any excuse, ever, for there being a blank day. But after twenty desultory minutes of taking photos of the ship's bell, I conceded defeat. There was nothing to photograph: I was cast adrift, and it was as if the earth was standing still.

There being no other course of action available, I sauntered along deck to seek refreshment with my laptop under my arm, exchanged a few insincere greetings with a couple of barflies and wondered idly what was to become of me. I must have been bored because before long I'd booted up my file management software and was tagging photos and deleting hundreds of superfluous images from the hard drive.

Inspired by such activities, I followed this up with cleaning all my lenses and reorganising my gadget bag. I even read my camera's manual and found out what some of those buttons you've always casually wondered about actually did. But for all the pride I was beginning to feel in conquering the nothingness, I really couldn't wait for something to actually happen.

5

Powerless in the
face of beauty

*Modern cameras are wonderful things, but they're not
much use if you leave a vital component back at base.
And yet there are times, especially if it's your day,
when good luck can turn up unexpectedly.*

Some time ago I wrote in my book *Travels in Search of a
Photograph* of an aborted expedition to Gower's Rhossili
Bay: an outing thwarted by an enormous tree that had
crashed down during an overnight storm and had brought
all traffic to a stop. And it was only recently that I was
complaining about how Christmas brings with it a tedious
lack of opportunity to get out into the field with the
camera. And so, as our most recent Boxing Day rose
bright and fair, a pale sun making stately progress across
the firmament in celebration of the abatement of the black
sheets of Christmas rain, the prospect of an afternoon trip
to Rhossili seemed to exorcise two of my demons in one

fell swoop. It was but the work of a moment to confirm with the local coastguard that not only were the meteorological conditions in my favour, but so also were the tide times, meaning that a hike across the causeway to the island of Worm's Head was on the cards.

As with my previous outing, I chugged along westwards in the automobile with a song in my heart. As I drove down into the valley at Parkmill, through which chuckles and burbles a jaunty little river called the Pennard Pill, I remembered with fond affection my previous ill-luck. Not today would there be an officer of the law bidding me to turn around and head back east. As I mused on such consoling thoughts, I threaded the car through the narrow lanes of the Lordship of Gower confident that today, of all days, would finally be *my* day.

I'd not planned to do anything particularly strenuous photographically, and so hadn't brought with me any equipment other than my regular, everyday workhorse camera that is usually to be found on my kitchen table. As it was already sporting one of my favourite wide-angle lenses, I was happy to just pick up the instrument and get on the road.

Having parked up near the Church of St Mary (where there's an interesting monument to Edgar Evans – the first of Captain Scott's men to perish on the *Terra Nova* expedition), I donned the Ray-Bans, set my sou'wester to an angle of seasonal jaunt, laced up the walking boots and set forth, if not quite like my fellow Welshman Henry Morton Stanley as he sallied forth to find Dr Livingstone, then at least with a sense of purpose that put the previous day's marathon of walnuts, port and junk TV to shame.

Here I was, a Romantic solitary at one with his natural environment and all was well. Indeed, as Julian of Norwich might have said, "all manner of things shall be well", and you can't get much better than that. And, it really has to be said, things were going to the point of spiff. That is, until I came across my first puffins.

Characterised by comic antics and a bizarre collective noun, my first 'improbability' of these photogenic little birds seemed to be noisily indifferent to the fact that my camera was completely and utterly stone dead. Of course, it was only the work of another moment to remember that I'd left the instrument's battery charging in the kitchen. I didn't have my gadget bag and consequently no spare, and so perhaps the most positive thing I could say at this point about the afternoon's entertainment was that I'd taken my camera out for a nice walk.

There really is nothing like being without a functioning camera to make you see the photographic possibility in everything. Before me were seals bobbing in the slate grey, salty waters of the English Channel. The air was stuffed with skuas and guillemots, gulls and petrels. The sun was dipping towards the horizon behind a ghostly skein of silvery silk. Nothing could have made the scene more perfect for a spot of Boxing Day snapping: apart from, that is, a battery. Here I was enjoying, as William Wordsworth might have said, that earth has not anything to show more fair, and yet I was literally powerless.

"How's it going?" enquired a voice at my shoulder. It was my old chum Joff taking the hound out for a walk. Now, I know this looks like a literary artifice I've concocted to save the day, but what follows is really what happened. As we picked our way over the mussel beds towards the Worm, I told him my tale of woe. "But your camera has a flash card in it?" he wondered. "Well, yes," I said before explaining that it was of hardly any use if I couldn't get the camera to work in the first place.

Don't you just hate it when someone says 'aha' and then solves all your problems with a straightforward piece of clever-dickery? He didn't, as you are supposing, produce a fully charged battery out of a top hat. But he did offer to lend me his spare camera, which he retrieved from his gadget bag with what appeared to me to be an undisguised flourish. As I removed the flashcard from my dead camera and inserted it into Joff's spare, he gave me a penetrating stare, eyebrow arched, as if you say: "Are you sure you write about photography for a living?"

After which we spent a wholesome and uneventful afternoon photographing Worm's Head – we even bagged a sunset shot of the Devil's Bridge – and though I say so myself, some of my photographs weren't half bad. And my friend had taught me a valuable lesson that I don't think I'll forget in a hurry. That's because once the cars had been put away for the night and we were finally celebrating St Stephen's Day in the way God intended (with a pint of Welsh beer), he taunted me endlessly, while I repaid his kindness by settling the bar bill.

6

Getting the monkey
off your back

A visit to one of Africa's least known tourism destinations
shows that there's more to photographing wildlife on the
Dark Continent than following the Big Five around in a
four-wheel drive. What about snapping some baboons?

I've not had a lot of luck with baboons. Over the years,
experience has led me to the conclusion that they are
disagreeable, confrontational, seditious creatures that
scavenge and steal. Of course, it's a huge mistake to
anthropomorphise animals (especially, it seems to me,
when they are from the primate order). But, in the spirit of
speaking as I find, it's difficult to think of them as
anything other than the animal kingdom's equivalent to
those intensely irritating hawkers you find in African
markets, whose only mercantile tactics are to beat you
into submission by hassling you to within an inch of the
limit of your patience. Instinctively, I tend to think of

baboons not so much as photographic subjects, but more an inevitable sling or arrow of tropical travel. As I say, they're a bit intimidating, and as the urban acculturated mob no longer have any fear of humans, they've become ghastly and antisocial, and are to be avoided at all cost.

In the Gambia, hawkers rejoice under the name of 'bumsters', and so already we can see that this somewhat overlooked West African country – which is also the continent's smallest – might have more of a relaxed attitude to life. The megafauna seems to be of a lower-octane category too: with no Big Five to attract trophy-bagging snappers, the undisputed attraction is the birdlife. Because of its proximity to the equator and due to the fact that the country is essentially one long riverbank snaking its way into the interior, it is of course paradise for birds.

With more than six hundred species – with a bit of effort you can see a third of them in a day – it's hardly surprising that the toggers you encounter on the road tend to have long lenses slung over their shoulders. TV presenter Chris Packham is one of the great wildlife ambassadors for the country: his influence as an enthusiast and advocate for Gambian birdlife means that a healthy twitching and snapping industry is starting to emerge, in my view with some justification.

Bird photography has never been what those tedious management consultants might describe as one of my 'core competencies'. But there comes a time in your life when there's everything to gain and nothing to lose. After all, as the subtext of the few Gambia guidebooks you can get hold of seems to imply, if you can't get good bird images here you might as well go back to the drawing board. So on my first morning, with the mist still swirling in the long damp grass, I prepared to feel once again like a complete novice. It's not such a bad feeling: there's always something to learn.

I was nonetheless harbouring the regret that I was in Africa and not photographing elephants when I came across a troop of baboons, preening and squabbling in the cool of the morning. Not those nasty food-stealing, spitting, aggressive primates that I described earlier, but a beautiful community of guinea baboons, burnt orange and bronze in colour, basking in shafts of golden light. Completely uninhibited by my presence, they went about what I now realise to be their real business, which seemed to me to be to organise their harem, while the juveniles half-heartedly wrestled or took things easy. I confess to never having seen anything like it in the realm of this species of Old World monkey, and according to my guide neither would I ever again, unless I were to return to this tributary bank of the Gambia River. As with the penguins of Antarctica or the iguanas of the Galápagos, it wasn't that the troop was ignoring my presence. To a man, they were utterly oblivious: their indifference derived from the fact that these individuals had never experienced the need to be afraid of, or steal from, humans.

There are in our existence spots of time that require no second invitation to understand the importance of what is before us. And I duly set to work recording the social groups, individual behaviour and, I cheerfully admit, the sheer fun of working so closely with such enchanting creatures. As the sun climbed and the temperature rose, the troop made ready to retreat into the forest and within five minutes they'd vanished thither and were gone. A fine morning was had, and all that was left for me to do was to transfer the images to my laptop in the scorching heat of the afternoon while the rest of the world rather sensibly took forty winks.

You know that feeling when your photographs aren't quite what you'd seen in your mind's eye? It's not that you blew the shoot or what you have before you is terrible. It's just not quite right for reasons you can't quite put your finger on. In my startled enthusiasm, had I made some bad technical decisions? Was I just not firing properly because some days that's what days are like? Whatever the reason, I didn't like the portfolio in the way I had hoped, and so resolved to shoot the whole thing again at the next opportunity.

My second invitation presented itself with the rising of the sun the following morning. My subjects were just as aloofly compliant and I walked away an hour later triumphant, with everything I needed, including a much-improved attitude towards baboons. Now, for the first time in my career I can claim to have some decent primate imagery on stock, meaning that by the time I'd boarded my plane and was heading for home I was a happier man than when I set out

7

Cold weather photography?
It's a dog's life

Nothing could be finer than a day's shooting in Canada's
wild interior, propelled along the trail not so much by the
internal combustion engine but a pack of Arctic dogs.
Inevitably, the enterprise was not as easy as it looked.

Oh, to be in Canada now that spring is here. Well not
quite spring, but as I stepped out into the glorious
February forests of Quebec, I couldn't help messing about
with that most famous of lines from Browning. The air is
crisp, the snow as white as paper, while the cobalt blue
skies are, well, sky blue, only in a way that makes you
think this might be the first sky you have ever seen in
your life. If you don't fall in love with Canada's great
outdoors there's something wrong with your soul.

Not quite spring, because it's 30 degrees of mercury
below. When the wind gets up, you feel more like Apsley
Cherry-Garrard and his chums on *The Worst Journey in*

the World down in the seldom trodden reaches of Antarctica, rather than a hiker heading for the interior with a couple of energy bars and a bag full of maple syrup candies stuffed into the pocket. But cold aside, this is Eden, Narnia and Arcadia rolled into one, where the grand, majestic landscapes beckon and your mind echoes to those long descriptive passages in Jack London's *The Call of the Wild*. The wilderness calls you and it is a strong call, and you must obey.

The Arctic dogs get extremely excited. Clever, muscular and brimful of enthusiasm, they bay to be clipped to the harness, and soon we're making ready to sled across the frozen lake at Sacacomie, flanked by great pine-clad mountainsides, camera poised for action. There's only one rule when dogsledding: keep both hands on the rail that connects you to the sled and both feet on the brake if you don't want to go anywhere. And so, fiddling with one of the dials on my camera with only a perfunctory connection to the vehicle, the six strong dogs, clearly hearing the cry of *'Allez, allez, allez!'* in their heads, set off like thunder rolling down from the Appalachians. Suddenly, and without ceremony, my world turns upside-down, my camera is about twenty feet away from me and, if I haven't quite let slip the dogs of war, there's certainly plenty of havoc to cry about.

As it turned out, this was but the first and by far the least of my problems. I might have mentioned that these snow-hounds are nothing if not enthusiastic and, as such, find themselves with little time for what I shall restrict myself to calling 'bathroom protocol'. They do their business on the hoof, the resultant frozen deposits flicked up behind them as the team races along. The scarf wrapped around my face is not so much a defence against the icy air, but an essential barrier to prevent one of the most unpleasant sorbets the world has to offer from making unwanted transit into the digestive tract as you rapidly gulp down huge lungsful of air from the labour of sledding. I was on the point of wondering what might be the best way to clean my lens when, completely out of the blue, it started to rain. With it came a new headache, only this time related to the phenomenon that scares all photographers more than half to death: that of the entanglement of water and electronics.

I suppose I was lucky in that my camera didn't completely give up its ghost until we were heading home in the failing light and penetrating frozen drizzle of a long day. We unclipped the dogs and trudged back to the Land Rover with the quiet satisfaction of a job well done, the canines gleefully peeing in the snow after a heavy stint of doing what they were put on earth to do. As the unpleasant mixture of ice and dog residue started to thaw on my clothes, I couldn't wait to get back to the lodge to be hosed down. As the wheels of the car crunched through the snow, I decided to take a sneak peek at my photos on the back of the camera. But the butcher's bill was that there was no sign of life in the machine.

Only time will resurrect a waterlogged camera, and as I waited, I felt a strange affinity with Dr Frankenstein as the modern Prometheus makes his monster come alive. The first flickerings were unpromising: a screen of unrecognisable computerish junk that bore more than a passing resemblance to a malfunctioning Space Invaders machine of yore. Menus spontaneously appeared and disappeared, the camera shut down, the camera booted up. Lights flashed and dimmed.

Somewhere in the innards of this electronic snowstorm were the images I had taken earlier. I also started to feel some sympathy with Wordsworth when he casually wondered whither is fled the visionary gleam. Sitting in the bar of the Sacacomie Hotel, and several glasses of

Malbec later, my camera slowly started to come back to life and appeared to be behaving itself. But it had been a close-run thing.

Oh, I forgot to mention the photographs. For the record, they were quite good, I thought, in that mildly detached way you sometimes get, which means you are barely daring to admit to yourself that there are some real barnstormers in the portfolio: a handful of images that made the whole adventure, though a lot more difficult than I had anticipated, worth the effort. A hard day out in the field, frozen to the bone, wet to the skin and covered in… well, you get the picture.

8

Desert island
discussions

*Being marooned on an island in the Middle East during
an unseasonal thunderstorm provided an opportunity to
reflect on how deficiency of imagination is making
competition photography more convergent than ever.*

A friend of mine, who is a thriller writer and therefore
cleverer than most on the Clapham omnibus, once told me
that he thought he knew how the world was going to end.
"As I see it," quoth he, "if and when the day comes for me
to make my appearance on *Desert Island Discs*, my first
choice of music will be the theme of the radio programme
itself. You can see the world disappearing that way, can't
you?" Indeed, I can, came my reply, for it is foolish to
disagree with a man who eats more fish than I do.

Let's suppose for a moment that there are readers not
familiar with the broadcast under mention. It works like
this: a person of note will imagine that he or she has been

cast away somewhere in the Seychelles or the Maldives or somewhere like that, with nothing more than an old-fashioned gramophone record player – one of those horn-shaped things that dogs bark at – along with a selection of records, the Bible and the complete works of William of Stratford. (For those of you wondering what a 'record' is; it's a 12-inch diameter circle of shellac, across the surface of which is cut a single spiral scratch from the outside circumference to the middle. When united with the gramophone player's stylus and rotated clockwise at a pre-determined speed – quite often 33rpm, but there are others – the combination of what is effectively analogue software and hardware reproduces an audio wave and the dog barks. It's a bit like an MP3 file, only more fun.)

This is something of a roundabout way of getting to my photographic reflections on desert islands. Although it may not immediately appear to be the case, human beings behave differently on islands and strange things happen to the photographer in particular. Don't take my word for it. I was once having a pint of the brown and frothy in the metropolis with Paul Theroux when, out of the blue, the travelogist declared that people who live on islands are routinely 'up to something.'

He has a point. As a Briton I find islands fascinating and the smaller they are the better. In the Lake District, retracing the events of one of my favourite boyhood books – *Swallows and Amazons* – I somehow managed to leave my camera on an uninhabited islet no bigger than a cricket square, only to find on my return the following day that it had gone. Off the west coast of Zanzibar there is the blissfully isolated island of Chapwani, which I sailed to at great effort and expense only to find that I had left my camera back on the mainland at my hotel.

But I don't think that these minor slings and arrows count as any great revelation about how islands work. As

I write, I'm sitting on a hotel balcony in Doha, the capital city of Qatar. The hotel is built on a man-made island of reclaimed land. The powers-that-be, in their wisdom, dug up a chunk of the desert that was in the middle of nowhere (and consequently worthless) before redeploying it to expand the coastline, which is some of the most valuable real estate on earth. Sitting here on my desert island I've not taken a photo for three days because it is raining for the first time in three months. This reminds me of a time a few years ago when stranded on Sir Bani Yas Island, off the coast of Abu Dhabi, the heavens opened and down came hailstones ranging in size from mint imperials to golf balls. No-one in the United Arab Emirates alive that day had ever seen hail and I spent many hours explaining to my hosts that, while not exactly standard weather where I come from, I was reasonably certain that we were not experiencing, as they supposed they were, the end of the world.

As the rain falls, I am given to thinking as to whether there is a photographic equivalent to the legendary radio broadcast. Beyond the fact that there were once several famous poster photographs in the 1970s that everyone had stuck to their student digs walls, I don't immediately suppose there is. And yet thinking a little deeper into the proposition, one thing that is frequent and infuriating about the programme is that the guests, in their self-aggrandising efforts to come across as more intellectually lofty than they are, or in their embarrassing attempts to appear to have down-with-the-kids street cred, seem to end up choosing the same pieces of music.

In that respect there is a Venn diagrammatic intersection between the programme and photography. Of course, there is: just as the guests recycle the same old tunes, our photographic competitions recycle the same old images. New and emerging generations of photographers try to buck the trend, while new and emerging judges try to buck the trend too. But both, it seems, are stuck in a groove not entirely dissimilar to our spiral scratch earlier.

To our credit, we occasionally make the effort to at least try to break out from these self-imposed parameters, and many of us do this quite successfully, at the expense of our ability to win competitions. But for the most part, when I see a portfolio of winning entries, I just wonder what records the toggers responsible will take to their island to go with their book of the Bard and the scriptures. Could anyone do anything as original as pick the theme tune to the show? Not in this lifetime, because that's the way the world ends.

9

By Endurance
we photograph

*As aficionados of the history of polar exploration mark
the centenary of Ernest Shackleton's doomed, and yet
triumphant, Imperial Trans-Antarctic Expedition, it's time
to reappraise the great polar photographer Frank Hurley.*

Anyone with even so little as a passing interest in the
history of the exploration of the Polar Regions will by
now realise that the Shackleton centenary is upon us and
sailing full steam ahead. Quibblers will question why it is
being celebrated in 2016 when the legendary explorer was
born in 1874 and died in 1922. The answer is that since
these dates fall outside what's these days considered to
constitute the 'Heroic Age of Antarctica Exploration', it
makes more sense to concentrate on the extraordinary
Imperial Trans-Antarctic Expedition 1914–17, in many
ways the closing chapter of the era. That expedition has
acquired the informal moniker 'Endurance' after the ship

that sailed the 28-strong crew, commanded by Ernest Shackleton, to the White Continent.

Originally called *Polaris*, three-masted barquentine was renamed after the Shackleton family motto *Fortitudine Vincimus* or, in common parlance, 'By Endurance We Conquer'. As is well known, *Endurance* was lost in the Weddell Sea before the expedition had achieved any of its objectives, crushed by the southern pack ice, and in so doing triggering one of the most desperate and noble rescues of the 20th century. The relief mission was described to me by the first man to set foot on the summit of Mount Everest, Edmund Hillary, as 'the greatest survival story of all time'. Official expedition photographer Frank Hurley was there to record it.

Most of us will recognise at least some of Hurley's work. In spring 2016 the Royal Mail commemorated the expedition by issuing a set of stamps, each image by Hurley, taken from large format glass negatives. Eight pictures trace the narrative of *Endurance*, from the moment the ship entered the ice to the climax of the story, when Shackleton returns south, victorious on the Chilean steam-tug *Yelcho* to fetch his stranded men. The tale that has been handed down is one of derring-do of *Boy's Own* proportions: the loss of the ship, camping out on the ice, arrival at Elephant Island and, last, the storied relief voyage of that much-modified lifeboat, the *James Caird*, that was to sail eight hundred miles across the stormiest waters of the world to raise the alarm.

Although there are plenty of stirring written accounts of *Endurance*, it is highly unlikely that the expedition would have remained in the imagination in the way it has, had it not been for Hurley's photographic legacy. Despite the fact that the 'Boss' (as Shackleton was known to his crew) and his boys were well and truly up a certain creek without a particular instrument of propulsion, the

Australian photographer carried on as if everything was all in a day's work. His apparent obliviousness to the inconvenience of being marooned (and in constant mortal danger) on the frozen shores of an otherwise uninhabited continent irritated other crewmembers, who noted in their diaries that he was also seemingly impervious to the unrelenting cold. Over the months, he created a portfolio of some of the greatest polar imagery of the epoch, only matched by the spectacularly gifted Herbert Ponting, photographer on Captain Scott's earlier and equally disastrous *Terra Nova* expedition.

Few who have seen Hurley's photographs will ever forget his haunting portrait of the ghost ship entitled 'The Long, Long Night' in which *Endurance*, fatally ensnared in the ice and looking like something out of the *Rime of the Ancient Mariner*, is picked out by twenty flashes against a jet-black sky. This sense of overpowering doom, of the futility of Man's struggle against indifferent fate, was later summed up in Shackleton's diary: "Where will we make a landing now? ... Time alone will tell." There are plenty of other superb shots by the maverick photographer who was the only member of the crew Shackleton stood in awe of. After all, the Boss was in Hurley's debt in that, although many other factors played a part, it was the rights to the still and moving imagery yet to be taken that had provided the collateral for much of the expedition's initial funding.

Hurley was above all a truly fantastic documentary photographer. While those around him were outwardly sanguine (while inwardly harbouring deep doubts) about their chances of successfully returning home, Hurley just got on with his job. He was often to be seen crawling in the rigging high above the decks in order to frame the shot he required, as he photographed every stage of the demise of *Endurance*. He photographed the camps that the crew struck on the ice after the ship sank, and followed the story through to Elephant Island, where on 15th April 1916 he even photographed several of the men enjoying their first hot drink on terra firma for more than a year. He also photographed the *James Caird* on many occasions: there's a cracking image of Shackleton's second-in-command Frank Wild overseeing the exhausted crew man-hauling her across the pack (a glorious print of which hangs on my kitchen wall to this day). There's one of her beached at Elephant Island in beaten and sorry condition prior to an ad hoc refit for the rescue voyage. Without these images, the story would just be words.

Famously, the crew of *Endurance* returned to Britain without the loss of a man. Shackleton fulfilled his contractual obligations by giving enormously popular illustrated lectures based on Hurley's photography. Meanwhile, the Great War was reaching its endgame and many of the crew dispersed to serve Empire in uniform.

Hurley's unswerving ability to do justice to historic moments wasn't diminished by his ordeal in Antarctica. His star ascended even further as he went on to shoot some of the most hauntingly memorable – and in some respects controversial – First World War photography in the European theatre on the Western Front.

10

The earth seen in
suspended animation

*For many of us the chance to do a spot of low-altitude
aerial photography from a light aircraft or even a
helicopter might seem to be the Holy Grail of fantastic
opportunity. But a hot air balloon something else...*

As with most of us, I don't often get the chance to see the
earth from above. As photographers, we routinely travel
the world seated beside scratched and foggy portholes in
the aluminium cigar-tube fuselages of passenger airliners,
maddened by the cacophony of kerosene-fuelled jet
turbine engines. But to get aloft in a lighter-than-air
balloon, wafting along on one of the most elemental of
scientific principles, seems to me to be the organic food
of the world of aviation. To drift in the light zephyrs of
the firmament, silently and without vibration, is one of the
great experiences in life. Not only that: it's a pretty good
way to take photos of the world as we so rarely see it.

Ever since I first saw that magnificent painting of a balloon's shadow on an empty beach sailing towards the open ocean, I have been spellbound by the possibility of a balloon safari of my own. The painting – simply entitled *Shadow* – first came into the public's imagination when it was reproduced on the cover of a popular anthology of contemporary poetry (edited by Andrew Motion, the man who was later to become Poet Laureate) that I read as an English Literature undergraduate at Oxford, way back in the misty recesses of the century before this one.

The artist was Michael Andrews who, with something of a photographer's eye, had produced a highly unusual and technically extraordinary image that, as with all the best paintings, asked more questions than it would ever answer. I couldn't possibly know where the balloon was going, but I knew I was going there myself.

And so to find myself in Egypt suspended over Luxor, held up by nothing more than a giant silk envelope of hot air, not tethered like one of those ghastly wildlife sight-seeing balloons you find all over the grasslands of Africa, but blown whither the wind willed, was something I never thought could be put into words. For those of you unfamiliar with what it's like to take to the air in a balloon, it is a ghostly experience in which the gondola does not so much rise, as the earth falls away.

In a helicopter you feel like a conker on the end of a string, tensely awaiting the next instalment of battle. But in a balloon, you feel like a bird, I suppose, if birds feel like this. I could hear the cattle lowing beneath on the banks of the Nile and smell the charcoal fires as coffee brewed in the cool of the misty early morning. Below, the majestic river's irrigated banks snaked through the Sahara like a green ribbon fluttering in the breeze, while above I clicked away, the sun low on the horizon, with the balloon casting a long shadow across the sands.

I'd been told that one of the great things about living in the villages beneath the flight path of the balloons heading for the Valley of the Kings was the continual harvest of sunglasses and cameras that fall to the ground from above. Although living an agrarian life of simplicity and economic modesty, the farmers who tilled the silty riverine fields all had Ray-Bans, expensive compact cameras, smartphones and iPods. In times of antiquity it once rained frogs and locusts. Today, it is electronic gadgets that fall to earth. "If it has a strap, put it around your neck and if it doesn't, put it in your pocket," warned my guide as I scrambled into to the open wicker basket. "Once you get in the air, things have a strange habit of jumping ship, and you'll never get them back."

It turns out that, while significant, the risk of losing your camera is chicken feed compared with the bigger picture. Before my departure for Egypt I'd been to seek advice from one of the most exciting balloonists of the modern age, polar explorer David Hempleman-Adams, who in 2000 famously became the first man to fly over the North Pole in a balloon, following in the footsteps of the ill-fated attempt by Salomon Andrée a century before.

Hempleman-Adams was also the first to cross the Atlantic in an open wicker basket Rozière balloon and has since broken endurance records in helium balloons. So, he's got the hang of it and knows whereof he speaks. His one bit of advice to me was related to the fact that once aloft, budding aeronauts cannot resist the temptation to climb out of the basket, under the impression that they are still on the ground. Given that this tends to happen at high altitude when the brain is starved of oxygen, you can see why Hempleman-Adams takes the precaution of tying his ankle to the basket interior with a sturdy rope. Given that my relationship with heights is at best rocky, I didn't feel that the polar adventurer had done much to encourage me.

And yet my aerial voyage was to be gentler than my adventurer friend was accustomed to. There was no drama, and nothing was lost. To float aloft, drifting past the ruins of a civilisation that never got to an altitude higher than a mountain peak or the apex of a pyramid, was a humbling experience. I came to earth with a bump, because there's no other way of landing a balloon.

Tumbling out of a basket that had been rudely dragged along in the sand seemed a small price to pay for an unforgettable journey. After a few moments, a four-wheel drive appeared and I was ferried back to my hotel, all the while anxious to see if my take on that famous painting was going to live up to expectations.

11

Picture-perfect poppies
of the Peloponnese

*When it comes to a foray into old-fashioned travel
photography, there are destinations that cannot possibly
live up to expectations. A trip to the rural reaches of
southern Greece, however, did not disappoint.*

Were I to write a list of the books I most loved as a child
it would be a long one I can tell you, as there were simply
so many. But what I can say is that I cannot imagine such
a list not including Gerald Durrell's warm and sumptuous
My Family and Other Animals, which propels itself to
somewhere near the top without doubt or delay. If I were
to write a similar list of favourite travel books, I'd have to
say that Patrick Leigh Fermor's *Mani* and *Roumeli,* for all
their overwrought writerly filigree, make their way to the
upper slopes with rapidity and avidity. And so it comes as
something of a surprise to me that of all the countries I've

been to over the years, I'd never been to Greece. That is until a week ago.

Filled with romantic notions of specimen hunting in the olive groves and literary excursions among the ancient ruins I was, I assured myself, without doubt destined for disappointment. It simply wasn't possible that rural Greece today could ever be quite as rose-tintedly beautiful and idyllic as these two vastly different, but equally brilliant, authors described it. As I was soon to discover, there is sometimes a certain pleasure in being proved wrong. As Durrell wrote: "spring had arrived and the island was sparkling with flowers."

My plane bumped through the last stratum of clouds towards the tiny speck of an airport in Kalamata in the southern Peloponnese, from which I could see the tawny-coloured mountainous landscape, looking for all the world as if someone had thrown a rather old and moth-eaten lion skin over a jumble of old furniture. Here was Greece in all its rugged splendour. Even as we made our descent, my cameras were practically begging to be set free from the gadget bag's dark interior.

Perhaps it is that mid-May brings with it a special spirit of the Mediterranean. Oranges and lemons, olives and jasmine, lizards and swallows. And everywhere in the parched meadows were flowers of gentle pink and white and yellow. But it was the red of the poppies that seemed so fierce and wild. It was as though that famous Renoir painting had come to life before my eyes. Such was the beauty before me I started to think that Durrell and Leigh Fermor might have in fact played down the epic grandeur of their adopted landscape. There is a Greek word for this: *litotes* is the epithet we give to the rhetorical device of literary understatement.

Although I'd done a quick reconnaissance mission in the air-conditioned comfort of a minivan with tinted windows, I was soon to discover that any exploration of the Peloponnese was better done on foot, but best done by bicycle. And so it was with more than a little of the spirit of those British expat authors whose first editions sit at home on book cases in the temperate maritime climate of South Wales, I set forth into the warmth of the Mediterranean, where the air was filled with birdsong, the buzzing of bees and the susurration of the breeze in the olive leaves. While snakes slid harmlessly along the deserted roads and eagles climbed steepling thermals, I set out to photograph poppies.

Perhaps there aren't so many invasive species of escaping garden plants in Greece, or maybe there's less monoculture and fewer modern chemicals to destroy their habitat, but poppies seem to flourish in this part of the world. Meanwhile in Western Europe, a flower that was once so hardy it could grow in the muddy trenches and battlefields of the Somme has now all but disappeared. It was an opportunity too good to miss.

With the sky a satisfying cobalt and the sea like lapis lazuli, I pedalled along through the realms of gold with a song in my heart, determined to take some of the greatest photos of poppies a photographer had ever taken. While in Flanders fields the poppies may well blow between the crosses row on row, and all that, giving a sombre air of remembrance, here in the cradle of civilization they have no such military association.

If anything, they speak of freedom and their wild beauty is intoxicating. Of course, none of this was lost on the classical poets of antiquity. Writing millennia before the Great War, Greece's greatest son Homer tells us of how Odysseus spent a decade fighting to return to his Kingdom of Ithaca, only a stone's throw from the Peloponnese. The great king *literally* went through hell to return to his homeland, as well as encountering the

Cyclops and the Sirens along the way. I can imagine Homer, as he invented ever more bizarre ways of testing and torturing his hero, quietly sitting under an olive tree chuckling conspiratorially over a goblet of retsina, surrounded by poppies.

The photos. I nearly forgot. Yes. Pleased to report they were everything I had hoped for, although nowhere near as good as some you could see when trawling the internet. But that's of no importance because when it comes to photography there's always something of the poet Keats' 'watcher of the skies' feeling you get when looking at other people's work, just as he had when he first read Chapman's translation of Homer.

No matter what you do, rather depressingly at times, someone has done it all before you, and more often than not much better. But in this case, it hardly mattered because sometimes – although by no means always, as we shall see in the following chapter – it's the journey that matters most.

12

Travelling light
through rain or shine

*From the ridiculous to the sublime... Two recent
photographic adventures of radically different objectives
and outcomes combined to remind me of one of the most
basic of all of the principles of outdoor photography...*

Threading my way through grid-locked, rain-soaked
Paris on the back of a motorbike, dangerously weaving
through fossilised queues of Renaults, Citroëns and
Peugeots, there wasn't much on my mind beyond
wondering if I'd make it through to another day. Although
I can't be certain, I think the issue of least concern at the
time was whether I'd brought with me the right gear for a
photoshoot commissioned by a British business magazine.

Let me explain. When the bell within the telephonic
instrument alerted me to the fact that there was someone
wishing to have discourse with me, and that the result of
the ensuing dialogue would be a commission to execute a

portrait of a boring software engineer on the other side of *La Manche*, neither party could have foreseen that the date selected for the venture would be the very one chosen by the GCT trade union (or General Confederation of Labour) to call an aptly-named general strike. The result was a woefully predictable meltdown of the transport infrastructure, the highlight of which was that there were no taxis to be had for love nor money outside Gare du Nord where it was raining cats and dogs.

Since my Eurostar had been badly delayed I was rapidly reaching the point where my time-slot to take the portrait was becoming but a thing of the past, and so in desperation I did the one thing you should never, ever do, especially in Paris, especially in the rain. I engaged a motorbike taxi. Fortunately I was travelling light – I had one camera, one lens, one battery and one data card – and after twenty minutes of the sins of my past flashing before my eyes, I disbursed to the sodden driver the eighty euros he required of me before rejoicing in the fact that I'd arrived to immortalise my subject an unfashionable five minutes ahead of schedule.

As I sat on the Eurostar later that day forging my way back to London, glass of Chablis to hand, I promised myself that my next assignment would be a more relaxing affair. After all, it was to be a trip to Tanzania where I'd been asked to photograph a swanky safari lodge for one of those luxury magazines that are hardly ever seen by the likes of thee and me because they have what's called 'private circulations'. Pouring another glass of what Keats called the 'blushful Hippocrene', I booted up the smartphone and skimmed the itinerary.

It's not easy to conceal your sense of bereavement when you read in bold, underlined letters in upper case that there is a weight limit to what you may carry of 15 kg. This is because in terms of photographic equipment, I think we can all agree, this isn't very much at all. But the reality is that once you've decided that you'll only take one change of clothes, you'll wear your hiking boots on the plane and that the accoutrements of human personal hygiene can be stripped back to a toothbrush with its handle snapped off, what you are left with is one camera and two lenses: one long, the other wide. Coincidentally, the camera body I took to Tanzania was the same as I had with me on that fateful day in Paris, but the lenses differed in that they were bigger and heavier. Even as I sat on the Piccadilly Line to Hades – I mean Heathrow – I was starting to get that nasty clammy feeling that told me I'd chosen the wrong equipment for the job.

Twenty-four bumpy, cramped and otherwise horribly uncomfortable hours later, I found myself ensconced in my temporary base deep in the Tanzanian Highlands, a stone's throw from the fabled Ngorongoro crater, where over the following days I intended to fill up my flash cards with elephant, eagle and wildebeest. As I sat under the veranda of the swish safari camp bar, idly watching the malachite sunbirds swooping in the twilight, I gazed at the pleasant beads of condensation trickling down the outside of my G&T. Before becoming too comfortable I decided to perform a rudimentary equipment check.

Thankful that the camera booted up and the lenses seemed to focus, and that data was making its way from the sensor to the card, I took stock. It had certainly been a risk to come all this way with just one camera body, especially as it had seen better days and further especially as one of its dials was in such a bad way I'd been forced to repair it on the road some while back with Blu Tack. Its exoskeleton is now a mass of cuts and bruises, and not for the first time I congratulated myself on the wisdom of having invested for as long as I can remember in metal-bodied cameras. Since all was well, I retired to bed of good cheer, slept like a baby, arose before the sun, drank deeply of the chilly African morning air and got to work.

Looking back on these two experiences – I'll leave it to you to work out which I preferred – I think that there might be, if not a lesson learned, then at least the reminder of a lesson all too frequently forgotten. And that is, you don't really need a lot of equipment to set the photographic process in motion. But you do need to get to your destination in one piece because, in an inversion of time-honoured conventional wisdom, sometimes it's the arrival and not the journey that matters.

13

Shooting the past through rose-tinted technology

There will be times when nostalgia for pre-digital technology leads to an overwhelming desire for a simpler life and a compulsion to go back to the drawing board. The camera obscura, however, is not the answer...

There comes a point in every man's journey through Shakespeare's 'Seven Ages' when, or so I'm told, no matter how hard we may try to resist, we will do daft things that seem out of character to the rest of the world. There will be those of us that drive around country lanes in roadsters or on Harley Davidsons, play Fender electric guitars that we should give to our children, or wear black leather jackets.

Not guilty, your honour. I have resisted the temptation to look ridiculous in exchange for reclaiming my lost youth, and I feel smugly entitled to a well-concealed air of superiority for so doing. And yet we all have a chink in our armour, as I discovered when I threw caution to the wind and on a whim bought myself a pinhole camera.

It may seem to be a small offence in a world where middle-aged businessmen routinely wear watches that cost more than my car, but it was an outrage all the same. Let me explain. I recently attended a weekend festival of folk music in the grounds of an old country house in Cambridge where, among all the fiddles, mandolins, lutes, hurdy-gurdies and dulcimers, there were artisans of traditional woodland crafts displaying their pre-Industrial Revolution skills. I met a man from East Anglia who makes a living from coppicing, a method of woodland management that has existed in England for thousands of years. Perhaps I should have said 'merrie England', because by the time I'd finished spoke-shaving myself a woodland creature out of hazel wood, I was living in an idealised topography of peasant revolts, maypoles, Robin Hood, real ale and, of course, Led Zeppelin.

As I bid my coppicer adieu, I realised that this extraordinary hankering for the roast beef of Old England could only be satisfied photographically were I to go back in time and do it the old-fashioned way. I'm not talking about dusting off my manual Leicas of the pre-digital era. I'm talking about going right back to the dawn of photographic time, when five millennia ago, a Chinese philosopher by the name of Mozi first observed an inverted image of a pagoda that had been projected through a pinhole. Yes, this was the technology for me, I thought, jauntily whistling a bucolic air from Gilbert and Sullivan, temporarily forgetting that our worthy Victorian operatists were in fact satirising the exact sentimental nonsense that seemed to be flowing out of me with guileless glee.

With a 'hey-nonny-nonny' and a 'fiddly-dee' I made my way to the camera emporium in Waterloo, where I disbursed sufficient coin of the realm to put me in possession of a wonderful little brown varnished box trimmed with brass fittings, before taking a steam locomotive (oh, all right, a crowded GWR train) down to Wales, where I would take my first pinhole photographs of Weobley Castle on the Lordship of Gower. By the time I'd signed the cheque, my new (or should I say 'old') camera was complete with roll film, a rudimentary viewfinder and even a rustic shutter release cable. It was so blissfully and innocently without complication it was hard to see what could possibly go wrong.

I write about photography enough to know that there are very few synonyms for the word 'photographer', and those that spring to mind seem either writerly or downright pretentious. There are only a certain number of times you can call the guy who depresses the button a 'togger', and as I soon found out, the epithet 'snapper' conveys a rapidity and efficiency that seems to have little or nothing to do with pinhole photography. As I ambled around the 14th century manor house on the Llanrhidian saltmarshes looking for my shot, words and phrases such as 'dither', 'procrastinate' and 'wading through treacle' sprang lazily to mind. Undeterred, I pressed on, certain that, having been inspired by some of the modern artists in the field, I would produce work of breath-taking, haunting, ethereal beauty.

I was wrong. For those who have never tried to take images with a lensless wooden box, allow me to explain that the process leaves you feeling completely powerless. You put the box on a tripod – I managed to find an antique wobbly brass one in a junk shop – make a few mental calculations, say 'um' a few times and then hope for the best. Not having a clue what was on the film, after about half an hour, I fetched up at an adjacent pub wondering what had just happened.

It was to be a week before I got my answer, when, looking at the contact sheet provided for me by what must have been an extremely baffled developer, I realised that the life of pinhole photography wasn't for me. I won't say that the images were badly exposed because that would imply that at some point I knew what went into exposing them correctly. I remembered ruefully the words of a photographer friend who had warned me over a pint in Soho's *Dog & Duck* that the art of the camera obscura was 'the definition of trial and error' and that it would take time to get the hang of it.

This is where I take issue with my friend, because I think what he really meant was that it would take *until the end of time* to get the hang of it. And time isn't on my side, I thought, as I peered enviously through the windows of the watch boutiques on Bond Street and the vintage car showrooms in the cobbled courtyards and mews of Mayfair.

14

Sri Lanka, where elephants aren't born free…

There can be few sights more depressing than that of a captive animal unable to obey its instincts, condemned to a life of boredom and distress. As photographers, it's our responsibility to do something about it. But what?

Most photographers have their favourite subject and mine is the elephant. To be precise, the African Elephant. Whether they be *Loxodonta africana* or *Loxodonta cyclotis*, it makes no difference: African elephants, to me at least, are the greatest of all wildlife photographic subjects and I love them. Maybe I'm one of the lucky few, but over the past decade I've had the privilege of photographing them in Tanzania, Kenya, Mozambique, Zambia, Botswana, South Africa and Namibia. I have photographed them on foot, from a camel, from a Land Rover, canoe, hot air balloon and even a helicopter. Every time I see one of these animals in the wild, I am inspired with the spirit of global optimism, and I am moved to long for a better and fairer world.

And so, it was with high spirits my daughter and I entertained the thought of encountering their cousin, the Asiatic elephant as they are now called, while labouring under the burden of a good old-fashioned summer holiday on the pear-shaped equatorial island of Sri Lanka. After unpacking and relaxing with a jug of mango juice by the hotel swimming pool, we threaded our way to the southernmost point of what Marco Polo deemed to be the finest island in the world. At Dondra Head there is a magnificent lighthouse from the top of which, if you look due south, you'll see nothing but the rollers of the Indian Ocean, beyond which the next stop is Antarctica. It's a wonderful place from which to consider the glories of the planet we live on. As we ambled peacefully the mile or two it takes to get to the town centre, where we intended to take a tuktuk back to base, we decided to go to the local temple to take a few souvenir snaps for the family album. Now, I wish we hadn't.

In the temple gardens we were greeted by the sight of an adult male *Elephas maximus* chained by its feet – I'll repeat that, *chained by its feet* – to a concrete plinth, displaying the sort of stereotypical repetitive behaviour that you see in zoo animals. My daughter, despite being only 11 years old at the time, was visibly shocked. She's a vegetarian, an animal rights supporter and a member of the RSPB. She asked me if there was something we could do to help the animal, and so after a minute or two I told her we should write to the Prime Minister of Sri Lanka to voice our disapproval. At the time, I somewhat carelessly thought that would discharge my responsibility.

The problem is that no matter how strongly we feel about these issues, it's not enough to simply stamp the feet and say that something should be done. For three reasons. First, as guests in a developing country, it is simply colonial to criticise the way it is run. Second, and here is the awful hypocrisy of such a stance, it was our occupying forefathers that caused such bloody terrible environmental damage to what was then Ceylon, it's a miracle here are any elephants left. They systematically cleared the montane forest to make way for coffee, and later tea, plantations, after which trophy-hunting British army majors massacred the elephants in their thousands.

Third, even if a campaign to free temple elephants were to succeed, what would be the unintended consequences? If these damaged creatures were, with the best will in the world, shunted off to a National Park such as Yala for a better life, it's by no means guaranteed that they'd reintegrate into the wild properly. Further to which, a visitor to another country can have no real insight into the economic role such temple 'attractions' play in local communities. If the village were to lose a crucial source of income, it's not hard to see a future where the local children, through force of economic necessity, found themselves working in sweatshops for a dollar a day, making school uniforms and footballs for our own kids.

You may well be wondering what all this has to do with photography. Well, it's like this. It's my view that as photographers we are among the top tier of global ambassadors for just about every environmental concern on the table. Of course, the scientific community plays a valuable role in coming up with the data that provides the evidence that can influence policy. But as a wildlife photographer friend so eloquently explained to me recently: "If science is the brain of conservation, then photography is its heart."

We all know the power simple imagery has to tap into the emotions of the human on the Clapham omnibus and transform general opinion. If I were to illustrate this chapter, I'd publish one of my shots of a glorious wild African elephant bulldozing through the swamps of the Okavango Delta. Beside it I'd print a photo of the temple elephant at Dondra, depressed and in chains. Underneath, I'd write the caption: 'Which is better?'

Later in our holiday we went to Yala, where my daughter and I photographed wild elephants in the far distance, doing what wild elephants are supposed to do: stomping about and having fun. We also visited a dreary 'orphanage' at Pinnawala, where a large herd of so-called 'rehab' elephants are at least given the opportunity to splash about in the river for a few hours a day.

As photographers I think we can make a change for the better here. Only don't get cross with Sri Lanka. Although it might sound more than a little holier-than-thou, we decided to write our letter after all. But instead of being all western-hemisphereish about it, we politely asked the government what plans it had to provide their elephants with a better future, and if we could get involved in some way. Maybe that's how photographers help.

15

Life's a camera.
Time to step inside

*There are times when you'll find the oddest of cameras
in the most unlikely of places. On the road to Jerusalem
there's an old abandoned pillbox that's been converted
into a pinhole camera by an enterprising local artist...*

Many photographers I should imagine will at some time
feel the call to travel to Jerusalem, to walk among the old
stones of scriptural history. As with Geoffrey Chaucer's
pilgrims, when spring comes with its sweet zephyrs, we
are compelled by the urge to go on pilgrimage. While the
mediaeval poet's dramatis personae took the more modest
route from Southwark to Canterbury to visit the tomb of
St Thomas Becket, I went the whole hog by travelling to
what was once thought of as the centre of the world.

You can't blame the Wife of Bath and her companions
for stopping short of the Holy Land: back in the 14th
century it would have taken the intrepid wayfarer two

years to get from Blake's green and pleasant land to Jerusalem. I did it in half a day despite having to negotiate the conspicuously un-pilgrim-like hordes of smoking, overweight package tourists that infect Luton Airport, the casual hostility of a bucket airline and all that goes with it.

And yet I felt something of the holiday spirit as I took a taxi inland from Tel Aviv to what some call the world's greatest city. After all, whatever your spiritual views might be, there's something undeniably uplifting about the prospect of walking through the backstreets of the Bible. As I made my tour of the Old City, visiting the Room of the Last Supper (that isn't in any factual sense the Room of the Last Supper), weaved my way along the Via Dolorosa (that isn't the original Via Dolorosa), and gazed in awe upon the empty Tomb of the Messiah (that probably isn't the empty Tomb of the Messiah, no matter how awesome), I was overwhelmed by the idea that this sort of experience is as much about what we want it to be as anything else. As I was on assignment for a luxury travel magazine, I took all the predictable 'shopping list' shots required by my picture editor with the easy air of a man who couldn't quite tell whether he was working or having the time of his life.

My first evening in Jerusalem passed in the manner that I have come to recognise most first evenings on the road passing in: unpacking, downloading and checking out a local bar or two. While becoming acquainted with a glass of local Israeli wine, the kindest epithet to which you can apply is 'interesting', I flicked through my itinerary for the next few days, intrigued to find that the following morning brought with it a visit to a military pillbox. Further reading revealed that, built in 1936 during the British Mandate period, its purpose was to act as a fortified lookout tower (that was really a rather blatant sniper's nest) along the road from Jerusalem to Gaza.

Today, that road is a busy thoroughfare clogged with cars and buses at rush hour, threading their way through respectable suburban Bauhaus apartment districts. To look at photographs from eighty years ago, it's easy to see how the area has changed radically. A black and white shot by an unknown hand shows that it was once scrubland with only a few buildings punctuating the landscape. One of these is the pillbox in question, sternly overseeing all before it. So it came as something of a surprise to find it today surrounded by a children's playground, hidden away amongst a few shady cypress trees. Painted in two-tone pastel green, the cylindrical two-storey tower now has a kindly aspect to it.

The reason for my visit to the corner of Tchernikovsky Street and HaRav Herzog Street thankfully had nothing to do with shooting people. Abandoned and under padlock-and-chain for decades, the pillbox has become something of a landmark, and the locals, my guide told me, regard it with affection and have long wanted to look inside. This year the authorities finally applied the bolt-cutters as part of their 'Open House' programme, in which abandoned buildings were given over to unknown young artists to display their work to the public. Photographer Shabtai Pinchevsky decided to go one better, and while he was happy to show me some of his recent images in the ground-floor gallery, he was even happier to invite me to climb the metal ladder to the first floor where he'd blacked out the embrasures to create a darkroom.

In one of the blanking plates, through which once pointed a machine gun, he'd drilled a tiny hole for taking photos of the scene in the valley below. No lens, just an old-fashioned white screen made from a linen sheet on the opposite side of the camera obscura, where we watched inverted projections of commuters making their way to – or is it from? – Jerusalem.

Shabtai explained to me the thinking behind his installation and in the idealistic words of a young artist, he deconstructed for me the shift in purpose of the reclaimed watchtower. He seemed to like the fact that today the 'shooting' is benign, and that the space has been redesignated for the pursuit of artistic over militaristic endeavours. He also seemed pleased that he was being visited a British journalist who understood what he was trying to achieve.

"Yes," he says, "we're actually standing inside a camera. Isn't that cool?" I reply in the affirmative, for it is indeed extremely cool to stand inside the chamber of a camera, watching real-time images of everyday modern life flickering by with a rudimentary resolution that wistfully evokes a distant world from the past. Perhaps not so distant after all, because everything in nearby Jerusalem's Old City seems to be so very ancient.

16

Getting to grips
with digital retro

*In a world becoming ever more obsessed with retro
styling, it seems that even the forward-looking pastime of
photography is following the trend by giving our work the
surface finish of what we once called the Good Old Days.*

Something very strange is happening. You can't pick up
a magazine these days without seeing modern images
presented as daguerreotypes, lithographs or wet plates.
Recently I saw a portrait of the legendary, but still very
much alive, Formula One driver Mika Häkkinen printed
on the pages of a luxury rag in sepia, where the image in
question appeared to be scratched and stained, with the
film rebate left on. It was as if I were looking at the great
man's grandfather rather than a chap who'd last won the
World Championship less than two decades ago. The
effect was to say the least arresting, if only because of its
incongruity. But the jaw ceased to drop in due course,

because it only took a moment to reach the conclusion that what I was looking at wasn't an authentic image shot on vintage equipment, but a software edit of a perfectly straightforward digital portrait.

Nothing wrong with that. Also, as with all good portraits this one stayed in the mind. The artist had caught the driver nicely and there was something about the interaction between the subject and his photographer that led to questions rather than answers forming in my mind. The deliberate choice of retro styling had been a good one by whoever took the creative decision – I don't know if it was the photographer or the art director – because it seemed to capture something: what those of us over a certain age would call the *zeitgeist*.

I use the word carefully because being deliberately old-fashioned these days seems to be something that is counterintuitively cutting edge. I won't bore you with my personal opinion of those dreary idiots that go around with Henry VIII beards calling themselves 'hipsters'. But they do represent a hankering for the past, and whether we like it or not, the external visuals of a bygone age are back with us and the choice is ours to either embrace the trend or to resist.

I don't know what psychologists have to say about this, but I think it's almost certain that they'd agree with me when I say that nostalgia is part of the human condition. A compound loan word from the Greek that literally means 'pain for home', nostalgia is the harmless condition that gives us (usually) groundless prejudices in favour of, say, vinyl 33rpm records over CDs, Wurlitzer jukeboxes over iPods, Duesenberg automobiles over the Prius Hybrid. You can see where this list is going... after a few more examples, I'm inevitably going to finish with the dramatic resolving climax, which will be 'analogue over digital.'

Quite right too. As humans we don't like to think that we've never had it so good, because what we are conditioned to thinking is that the Good Old Days were better. But with photography this is where you hit a bit of a snag, because when we think about old photos, in general we look blindly at the world through rose-tinted spectacles. That is because the photographs we take today are miles better than they used to be. That's not necessarily because we are better snappers, but because digital technology has given us limitless opportunity to refine, reshoot, recompose. There's no point saying that fragile expensive rolls of film yielding a measly 36 grainy images, unnatural in colour and soft as marzipan, were somehow better than a sensor and a flash card that can cut rectangles out of the world with mind-blowing fidelity. Because they weren't. In my past life as a magazine editor in the late 20th century, I spent more time than most in uncatalogued photographic archives, desperately looking around for prints, negs, transparencies and even lantern slides that weren't awful or in terrible condition.

What I will admit though, is that in the transition from those halcyon days of film to the prosaic yet perfect present, we lost something. And that something is the palette of minor imperfections that make what we do seem somehow more human. As absurd as it may sound, when the compact disc first came out, some artists and their producers, disliking the clarity of the sonic presentation that came from the playback monitors, added 'crackle tracks' – a layer of audio imperfection replicating scratches on vinyl – to make their recordings sound more authentic. There they were with the digital world at their feet, and all they wanted was their compact discs to sound more like, er, records. Which isn't a million miles away from the creative process going on behind the portrait of our Formula One driver.

Intrigued, I decided to delve a little deeper and before long had installed a photographic film emulator on my laptop. Then I did what everybody who has ever bought one inevitably does: I set about producing daguerreotypes, lithographs, collodion wet plates, calotypes and autochromes. And I was thrilled with the results. That is until I realised that I'd gone over the top. I soon realised that to have any chance of anyone taking anything I'd done seriously I'd have to dial it right back. In fairness to the software developer, there is a 'dial it right back' slider prominently positioned at the top of the screen. Now I just overlay the faintest suggestion of my favourite film from years gone by (such as Velvia or Portra) and the world seems to make more sense.

What have we learned? Well, to put it in as few words as possible. Humans are nostalgic. Nostalgia is deceptive. Listen to the past: just because some of us used to shoot on film, that doesn't make us idiots.

17
Cold comfort for a
camera crisis in China

*We may think that as photographers we live in a world
where life is one long leisurely stroll in the sunlit uplands
of peace and goodwill to all men. But there are times
when it all comes crashing in, and not in a good way.*

Of all the difficulties I encountered when I started as a
fledgling photographer by far the biggest – and I really
wish that I could say something more profound here –
was simply that of the sheer vastness of the financial
stimulus required to get things going. I've never been a
man overwhelmed by the burden of wealth, and so to find
my career stifled at the outset by a vulgar insufficiency of
cash didn't come as much of a surprise. Rather, it was the
scale of my fiscal deficiency that left me poleaxed. After
all, as a writer all I'd ever needed was a pencil and an
exercise book: items which are usually more than covered
by the remuneration of a schoolboy's paper round, or

easily stolen, I mean scrounged, from the office stationery cabinet. But photography requires tons of cash.

To be confronted by the prospect of the tools of my prospective trade being so wildly out of reach, and to be so woefully out of my financial depth, was to say the least a bit of an eye-opener. I know that established and annoyingly wealthy exponents of the art like to lean on the bar and tell you their highly polished tales of how it's not about gear, but vision, determination and guts. But the fact is that without the unforeseen bequest of a hitherto unknown maiden aunt with a tumbledown country house in Kent, you're unlikely to walk out of a swanky London camera boutique with anything other than a sense of humiliation. It took me years of sacrifice to get all the lenses I thought I needed. Now I only use two, I can safely say that I learned my lesson both the hard and expensive way.

The thought of losing any of my gear while on the road is too much to bear. And although my career has been relatively free from disasters of this nature, I have had experience of being on the road with another togger when, at the end of the day, there was more metaphorical blood on the stage than the fifth act of a Jacobean revenge tragedy. Those of you who know me will know that I am of course referring to an ill-fated trip to northern China with my friend Bunsen, a formidable travel photographer, and yet, as we shall see, someone who does not enjoy a particularly close relationship with Lady Luck.

It must have been towards the end of the analogue era because as my friend and I dispatched a few glasses of something yellow, cold and fizzy on the plane to Beijing, we swapped stories about what we were going to do with our beloved medium format film cameras when the Digital Dawn finally kicked in. We both had experimental digital compacts, but neither of us thought a great deal of them and, to be honest, there was a consensus that while these things might be of some use to small children, the grown-ups would be still shooting on film until the end of time. We changed planes and headed north to Harbin, famous for its (brutally cold) annual ice festival and, being close to the Russian border, its caviar and onion-domed orthodox churches. We were, we agreed, going to have a lot of photographic fun, and we would return home to Blighty heroes, with bags full of film that when developed would propel us a rung further up the ladder out of the abysm of photographic obscurity and towards international stardom.

To those who have not been to the ice festival at Harbin I say this: you have brought upon yourself a photographic injustice that must be corrected immediately. Take all your cameras and head there as soon as you can. Only when you do, make sure it is after you've had a brace of wing mirrors connected to your shoulders. It all happened so quickly. Bunsen merely put down his gadget bag for a moment and had only turned his attention to his tripod for a second. But it was too late, and the bag had gone. As a writer, you're supposed to be able to describe things clearly and evocatively, but as the full force and effect of what had happened to my friend began to sink in, I realised that for all the purloined pencils and exercise books, I was at a loss. All I can say is that an evening spent in a Chinese police station, while the mercury is at minus 30, trying to explain what had happened to a desk sergeant who made no attempt to disguise the fact that he was loving every minute of our frozen despair, is not one I would ever wish to repeat.

Eventually, we gave up, sure and certain in the knowledge that not only had Bunsen's world been stolen from him, but there was also not a single insurance company in the world that would believe a word of what we had to say, much less dispense so much as a kidney bean in compensation.

As we sat in the bar of our hotel drinking Russian vodka and trying to warm up our souls, I opened my wallet and gave my friend every scrap of currency that was in there, with the words "This is to get you started again." As Bunsen looked at the pile of yuan that was probably worth no more than a flash card, we both burst out laughing, mostly because all other options were unthinkable.

18

Christmas in India was no photographic cracker

Force of circumstance occasionally means you've got to use cheap equipment. You can try to make the best of these things but, on holiday in India, I discovered that I might have been better off without any camera at all...

There are times when we all impose upon ourselves long journeys with tight schedules, but this was ridiculous. The idea was to travel non-stop from the biting cold of the Antarctic Peninsular to the comforting warmth of a sunset-facing beach in India.

The former was the location of an assignment for a national newspaper, where I'd been sent to photograph penguins and abandoned scientific research stations, while the latter was where I was to join my family to celebrate a once-in-a-lifetime tropical Christmas. For those interested in statistics, my voyage would involve four continents, one ship, five aeroplanes and countless long-distance taxis. But all would be well, because everything was planned down to the last jot and tittle.

The key to arriving in Goa by Christmas Eve was to do 'the switch' in London, where I'd briefly return to my flat, dump the polar gear and swap it for a pre-packed bag of Bermuda shorts and Hawaiian shirts, sandals and sarongs. As sun block and sunglasses were requirements of both adventures, the pit stop seemed to be a triumph of efficiency over a schedule that would put the fear of God into lesser mortals. I'd need to make snap decisions over what camera gear I'd leave behind. But as I have already said, the logistics were nailed down with the accuracy and ruthlessness of a military campaign. The last thing I was going to do was waste any energy on what could go wrong, because nothing could.

My ship duly docked in Ushuaia, the southernmost city in the world, on the very tip on Argentina's Tierra del Fuego. It was but a matter of minutes to clear customs and flag down a taxi that would take me to the somewhat bijou local airfield, from where I flew to Buenos Aires, changed planes and charged north to Madrid. In Spain, I sallied forth to Gatwick, where my pre-booked minicab awaited me. It was easier than picking apples off a tree and I was as confident as could be expected. If I were to descend into that abominable business of management jargon, I'd describe the whole affair as being one characterised by an abundance of low-hanging fruit.

"You've got a problem," intoned the driver a tad too gleefully for my liking. He'd been fully briefed over a beer or two before I'd set off to Antarctica and was ready to leap into action. "You see, there's a baggage handlers' strike at Heathrow, and people have been stuck waiting for their plane to take off for three days. They're even putting up marquees to accommodate the overspill queues." Thinking that this didn't sound too catastrophic, even for a dark snowy day in late December at the UK's busiest airport, I was brought back to earth when Desmond told me that what awaited me was a scene of "utter carnage. Probably no point even trying."

I internalised the word 'poppycock' with manly and British reserve, and as the driver sat in my kitchen drinking tea, I quickly grabbed what I needed from my polar kitbag and transferred it into my Globe-Trotter valise. "Don't bother with that," he chirped: "it's the guys with check-in luggage that are being held up. Your best chance is to arrive with carry-on only." Knowing that check-in clerks blanch at hand luggage coming in at more than 10 kg, I started to repack, this time under the gun. Metal-bodied cameras and telephoto lenses were out of the question, and so, with the seconds draining away, I decided to take my leather hat, passport and little else. I'd buy a compact camera for my family album snaps if I ever got airside.

What happened next was quick and efficient. We glided past the cohorts of simultaneously stressed and depressed holidaymakers outside Heathrow and, with nothing more than a backpack to slow me down, I breezed through check-in, security and passport control in something like twenty minutes. I was going to catch my flight and the Christmas reunion with my daughter was now a formality. I stopped at one of those electronics shops in the mall that never sell you anything you really need, unclipped the purse to the total of three hundred quid, and with my sleek new toy still in the box, munched peanuts all the way to Mumbai, snoozed through a short-haul to Goa, and chatted amiably with the taxi driver who spent the next four hours searching for my beach hut in the tropical sun.

After the longest journey I'd ever undertaken, and after battling with the sort of impedimenta that would have entirely defeated Greek mythological heroes, I arrived at

Mandrem Beach exhausted to be sure, but overjoyed to see my daughter sporting dolphin-like in the surf before a decidedly pleasant smoked salmon sunset. After greetings and salutations all round, I decided it was time to take some pictures. As my new unfamiliar compact camera sprang into life of sorts, I felt a wild pang of nostalgia for the proper instruments of the trade that were now taking a well-earned rest on my kitchen table in London.

The results were excruciating for exactly the same reason that instant freeze-dried granules, powdered milk and saccharine tablets won't make you a presentable cup of coffee. I tried to put a brave face on it. But as I made my tour of temple ruins, night markets and street cricket matches, I came to realise two things. First, there are times when you're better off simply not bothering to take any photos at all, and second, the adjective 'compact' has no place in my photographic vocabulary, and is better applied to cars, audio discs and political alliances.

19

Smartphone cameras and those wedding shoot woes

You wouldn't try to make a phone call from your top-of-the-range camera. So why should people think that you could take professional photographs with a smartphone? It's a daft idea that could spoil a perfectly good wedding.

Some years ago, I was sent on assignment to New York to interview Buzz Aldrin, and as if that weren't thrill enough, the magazine responsible for the commission had booked me into business class for the transatlantic flight. As such largesse is practically unheard of in the world of publishing these days, I assumed that a logistical mistake of some sort had been made and said so to the woman checking me on to the flight.

Subsequent to her reassuring me that there had indeed been no clerical error and that I should mentally prepare myself for 'turning left' upon boarding the plane, the expression 'yabba dabba doo' spontaneously leapt to mind, much in the way the noble salmon leapeth in the waterfalls of the Scottish glen.

The first and cardinal rule of flying long haul is never, ever under any circumstances whatsoever, engage in casual conversation with the stranger sitting next to you. And yet the woman to my left seemed pleasant enough for me to lower my guard and, as we quaffed pre-take-off champagne, I started to wonder if my dictum might be just a tad draconian. No such luck. I was right in the first place: the hours that followed seemed like days as Frangelica droned on about her forthcoming wedding to some poor unfortunate wraith, who seemed destined for a life of prolonged monologues on subjects too trivial to even contemplate. As with Coleridge's Ancyent Marinere she showed no mercy, verbally pinning me to the porthole as she soliloquised on her prospective matrimonial ceremony without hesitation, repetition or deviation.

What has this to do with photography, I hear you ask, and it is something of a good question. My travelling companion, having reached the point where she was starting to bore herself, wondered aloud (out of politeness more than any genuine desire to find out the answer) what I did for a living. And here comes the second cardinal rule of the long-haul flight, which is never to tell a stranger the truth about what you do for a living. As I watched the word 'photographer' float through the ether towards her, I knew I'd sentenced myself to further torture.

It is a very dark cloud indeed that bears no silver lining, and as my fellow passenger and I exchanged views on wedding photography, I started to realise that I'd judged too harshly a perfectly reasonable woman whose only crime was to be voluble on what was, after all, one of the days of her life. Furthermore, she didn't want to make the mistake that Charlotte and Tarquin had made when it came to their wedding photos. Turns out that Lottie and

Tarks had decided not to employ a professional snapper to capture their nuptials, being of the opinion that their guests, all of whom were in possession of the swankiest of smartphones, could record for posterity the whole gig in a frenzy of what we now have come to think of as 'citizen photography'.

"Was it a complete disaster?" I inquired with as much insouciance as I could muster under the circumstances. Totally, she confessed, before telling me that it had all started off swimmingly well, and that the day had been a day to remember, and everybody had shared their pictures on picture sharing social media platforms, and everything had 'looked okay' on the screen. Of course, the true scale of the debacle didn't begin to emerge until the newly-weds decided that they wanted printed copies of the photographs and started to encounter quality assurance issues related to resolution, sharpness, file size and so on.

But the real stinker was that the photos were basically rubbish. For two reasons: first, they were taken by people who weren't proper photographers, whose interest and ability in what they were doing declined in proportion to the quantity of alcohol consumed; while second, and here I need to quote my friend in full: "The thing about cameras on phones is they're not very good at taking photos." Add to that the fact that smartphones are no good at making audio phone calls either, and what you have on your hands is an expensive heap of electronic junk.

I use the last expression in a calculated manner because I think it's time someone stood up and said that the mouldy old cliché of 'the backward march of progress' could have been invented for the digital world. I know there are a million reasons to be grateful to the inventors of the integrated circuit, and that to live during these early days of the digital revolution is to be present at one of the greatest moments of mankind since *Apollo 11* delivered

Neil Armstrong and Buzz Aldrin to the Moon. But even the most diehard of advocates for the smartphone will at some time have to admit that, when it comes to serious photography, they are of no more use than a trinket from a Christmas cracker.

Of course, it is a wonderful thing to be able to review our images on a screen while we are working. And it is a wonder beyond all wonders not to be forever changing film, paying for development and waiting for processing. But we have to let common sense prevail at some point, and I think that when my airborne friend, in all her loquacious innocence, told me that smartphones make for terrible cameras, she hit the nail right on the head.

20

Waiving the rules
on the ocean blue

*We're always being told that we should take fewer photos
to allow more time for planning. But there are times when
acting on impulse can be better than actually thinking –
when you need to throw the rulebook out of the window...*

You may think that the expression 'carry on regardless'
doesn't have many applications in the world of travel
photography, and I would agree wholeheartedly. We are
of that rare breed of artist that not only lives by the adage
'less is more', but also understands why we do. And yet,
even the strictest of our clan depresses the shutter actuator
with all too depressing frequency and we show too much
work that we're not satisfied with to too many people. We
all do it, but for the most part we have enough self-
awareness to sometimes apply the brakes. We do not, as a
rule, deliberately carry on regardless, even if it sometimes
may appear so.

And so you may imagine my surprise when I recently became aware of the sub-vocalised imperative rattling around in my brain urging me to take more shots. This extraordinary state of internal affairs had been brought about by a concatenation of variables that overloaded my photographic brain to the point where the only thing I could think of was to carry on shooting. For those requiring more real-world data to flesh out what I'm describing, I was shooting some of the world's fastest 'boats' (not 'yachts') from a speedboat.

Looking back on my childhood, pottering around Swansea Bay in a do-it-yourself red-sailed Mirror dinghy, I remember sailing as something of a sedate affair, where the most notable mishap to befall me was the occasional clout over the back of the head from the boom when tacking, or maybe the odd capsision. I wasn't much of a sailor, I'll admit, not because of any lack of affinity with the ocean, but because I simply couldn't master the terminology. To this day, I find it difficult to differentiate between the jib and the mainsail halyard, my sheets from my stays, or a spanker from a spinnaker.

But this was different. I'd been sent out on assignment to Bermuda to cover the launch of the British challenger for the 35th America's Cup, a stern-looking charcoal-grey, carbon-fibre foiling catamaran that rejoiced under a name no more romantic than 'R2', sailing under the colours of Land Rover BAR. For those with an interest in such things, the three-letter acronym stands for Ben Ainslie Racing. And so, it was in the presence of Sir Ben, this country's greatest competitive sailor, I clicked away at the christening of the boat itself. After the formalities, a group of photographers was taken out onto the Great Sound racecourse to observe some of the other teams undergoing trials and testing. Land Rover BAR kindly lent us a speedboat, and so off we went into the sparkling Atlantic sun to get some shots for our newspapers.

The pilot was a nice enough chap called Phil, who seemed to care not one jot whether or not we donned the life vests that had been provided for us. He was far more interested in telling us how he'd sailed the Duke and Duchess of Cambridge around Bermuda only the week before on this very same vessel. But there were a few guidelines to follow most of which related to how close we could get to the race craft. For those of you who have not seen the 2017 incarnation of America's Cup boats, they are (to me at least) unconventional in that, instead of sporting cloth sails as in the days of yore, they now come with a single vertical rigid aeroplane wing that's as tall as five double decker buses stacked one atop the other. Because all the words are different, when the boats get going, they 'fly' on hydrofoils, lifting 99 percent of the boat clean out of the water, travelling at speeds of up to 60 mph (not 'knots'). Even before we had started, I didn't think that photographing them in action would be easy.

After we started, my supposition was confirmed as Phil, smashing bloke that he was, seemed more concerned with adhering to the strict official proximity guidelines for support craft, than getting us into a good position to photograph the vessels. We needed, I told him, to be upwind so that we could photograph them advancing towards us. We desired to have the sun somewhere behind us so that they wouldn't appear as black silhouettes in a whiteout sky. And we ought to shoot them while they were foiling, which meant that there would be a certain amount of keeping ahead required. It would also be great, I offered helpfully, if we could cut our engines from time to time to reduce the vibration of our own boat, because, well, photographing something that's moving from something else that's moving, with a long lens and all sorts of other impeding variables, meant that what we were doing was a bit more demanding than messing about on the river.

Two spray-soaked hours later and I was back at Land Rover BAR's swanky new Bermudian headquarters reviewing my efforts on the laptop. I won't say that what had happened made bird photography look easy, because nothing ever could, but as I sifted the wheat from the chaff, I was alarmed by the bias in favour of the latter. Hundreds of shots went straight into the digital trash, while a tiny proportion went into the 'possibles' folder. Keepers were few and far between.

But I got there in the end, and as I continued to edit my slender portfolio on the rickety old Boeing bumping its way back to Heathrow, glass of Bermudian Gosling's rum to hand, I pondered on what might have been had I listened to the idea that less is always more.

21

When photography
sings the blues

*If the reason for there being so many photographs today
is that photography is easy, then the reason there are so
few great photographs is that photography is also
difficult. Maybe a musical analogy will clear things up.*

One of the central paradoxes of photography is that it
should be simultaneously so blissfully simple and yet so
fiendishly difficult. It's something that has often occurred
to me, and yet I've never really managed to find a way of
articulating this contradictory proposition in such terms
that made it easier, rather than harder, to understand. That
is until a few days ago when, having a pint or two at the
local tap-house with a merry band of comrades, I found
myself, back to the wall, defending my thesis with a
certain amount of frustrated vigour. "What do you mean:
it's difficult and easy at the same time?" they chimed in
unison. I tried a few analogies on my non-photographic

friends, but to no apparent avail. Their counterargument, presumably drawn from experiences with smartphones, was that it was as easy as pressing a button. Furthermore, as with driving Formula One cars or being an astronaut, taking photos was a mere bagatelle and it was a deception to claim otherwise, and we were all being hoodwinked.

Just as you should never pick a fight with someone who buys ink by the barrel, you should never pick up gauntlets dropped by people who don't know what they're talking about. But I simply wasn't going to be put onto the canvas by such featherweight thinking. And then I got it. "Look," quoth I, "it's just like playing the blues. You can learn the nuts and bolts in no time at all. But you'll spend the rest of your life trying to play it properly". I'm not quite sure if the comparison is watertight, but it certainly had the effect of stopping my companions in their tracks. And while they returned to talking about how F1 was simply driving around in circles, I tried to disguise the look on my face that was inviting them to construct a meaningful sentence using the words 'pipe', 'stick' and 'smoke'.

As I have never been a man prone to swagger, I decided that it would be unfair to accept the victory laurels without at least first testing my idea in the context of practical experiment. Upon returning home, I duly dusted off my best guitar made by the worthy luthier C F Martin & Co, and got weaving. I decided that I would learn Blind Willie Johnson's *It's Nobody's Fault but Mine*, which he recorded on 3rd December, 1927. This for the simple reason that despite sounding quite straightforward, the song has earned a reputation for challenging the most gifted of musicians, including the mighty Led Zeppelin.

As I'm supposed to be writing about photography, I'll keep the next bit short. But in point form, once it's clicked that you need to retune your instrument from the standard 'Spanish' to D major, you have a simple 12-bar structure concentrating predominantly on the tonic, subdominant and dominant notes of the scale.

Providing you can play a guitar in the first place, you will certainly get the song into good enough shape to strum down the pub in no more than twenty minutes. The problem, as I found out, was that to get it any better than 'good enough for the pub' was virtually impossible. While I think we can probably all agree that Johnson was a genius with the bottleneck, whereas I am not, there is also something else going on here. That is because, if we switch back to photographic terms, I had got to the point where I'd understood all that stuff about shutter speeds and aperture, and yet not fully realised what it meant to take a photograph. In other words, I'd done the easy bit, which strange as it might seem, is precisely what puts so many off serious photography from the start.

They don't call it the blues for nothing. By the time I'd listened to Johnson a few more times I had drunk deeply of the desperation of this poverty-stricken blind preacher man, living in the shadow of slavery in America's Deep South during the worst economic depression the world had ever seen, whose only hope of salvation is that of reading the Bible. I started to wonder what it would be like to be possessed of a gift that could allow me to take a photograph as loaded with feeling and as hauntingly wraithlike as that song. And there we have it: only the camera is the guitar and the photograph is the song. How many cameras have we owned in our lives because it is easy to own a camera? And how few great photographs have we taken, because it is difficult to take a truly great photograph? Easy and difficult at the same time. Thus it was demonstrated.

As a footnote, Johnson recorded only thirty songs. But this was sufficient to ensure immortality. When his house burned down, he had nowhere to go and so carried on living in the ruins, eventually dying of syphilis, alone, unknown and unloved. To this day no one is sure exactly where he is buried.

But we do know one thing: and that is his music is literally out of this world. Along with recordings of masterpieces by classical composers such as Mozart, Bach and Beethoven, Johnson's gospel blues were cast into the cosmos on the *Voyager* spacecraft in 1977, with an accompanying message of peace to any civilisation out there capable of understanding it.

22
Lessons learned
from a flying bomb

The expression 'experience is the teacher of all things'
might well have been coined for the photographer.
After all, there isn't one of us that hasn't made an
embarrassing mistake that we can't learn from...

It was one of those old-fashioned late spring sunsets
when the air was full of blackbird song and, because we
were in central London, wailing sirens. Due to the
clemency of the evening, Hunter and I were sitting
outside Soho's *Dog & Duck* quaffing the brown and
frothy, swapping tales of life on the photographic road.
He's a successful and – if not quite a household name –
recognisable figure in the world of polar photography and
so, because of what follows, I have cloaked him in the
anonymity of a pseudonym. After all, you don't want the
photographic community at large to know that you're the
sort of bloke that goes around lighting fires in helicopters.

There was a reason for creating what he described as a 'flying bomb'. Hunter told me that the expedition team, of which he was official photographer, was flying north out of Resolute Bay, deep in the Canadian High Arctic, towards their drop off point five hours away.

These things are always about safety, my friend reassured me. But there comes a point when the sheer scale of the finances involved means you've got to take the occasional risk. Expedition helicopters are modified to save weight and stripped of their interior comforts to make space for supplementary barrels of aviation fuel. Of secondary importance, passengers are left to try to stay as comfortable as they can. Above the Arctic Circle, warmth is a relative concept, but once the eggbeater's rudimentary heating system had given up its ghost, 'relative' was turning to 'absolute'.

Finding his human cargo literally freezing to death, the pilot periodically landed on the ice to allow the team a few minutes to 'warm up' on terra firma. But it soon became clear to all involved that for every unscheduled landing, the chances of reaching their destination were diminishing dramatically. At this point a wonderfully elegant logic kicked in, leading the guys to light an open fire in the cabin. All seemed to go reasonably to plan until the pilot objected to a five-foot sheet of inflamed kerosene in his whirlybird and consequently invited the half-asphyxiated explorers to extinguish their improvised airborne bonfire.

"You really should write a book about your exploits," I volunteered, thinking this tale could be the first chapter in one of those unputdownable romps of the hapless adventurer. But Hunter wasn't so sure. "You see", he explained, "the problem is that while armchair explorers tend to revel in blood-curdling stories of cannibalism and frozen cameras, if you're going about your business properly, things like that hardly ever happen." He went on to say that in his twenty-five years photographing the Polar Regions, having reached various poles – north and south, geographical and magnetic – several times on foot, with dogs, by surface motorised transport and by air, there weren't enough 'juicy anecdotes' to fill up the inside of a birthday card, let alone a book. That's why he'd rather go quietly about his business and he'd be obliged if I repeated his 'fire in a chopper' saga to no one.

While I could see Hunter's point, his narrative had got me thinking. Can there be one of us that hasn't done something just a bit, well, daft in the commission of our photography? I'm probably a little less reticent than my polar friend in confessing my sins, but then again that might have something to do with my stories having more to do with innocent negligence rather than the downright risk to life and limb. I can clearly recall the several occasions when opening my gadget bag has revealed schoolboy errors bordering on farce. I'll freely admit that there has been more than one occasion when I have failed to pack spare batteries. And I'll cheerfully put my hand up to going out into the field with a camera comically devoid of a flashcard.

I've arrived at a shoot with the wrong lenses, while once I unpacked my gear to find that I was without a camera of any sort (although, in my defence, it had been stolen at that most notorious of international airports at Johannesburg). I've left semi-critical items – such as cloth backdrops, duct tape and polarising filters – in hotel rooms. But none of these incidents has ever put a project at mortal risk, and were I not writing about it in a context such as this, I would barely give such transgressions a second thought, beyond reminding myself to be more watchful in future. My more excruciating embarrassments seem to fall more into slightly less serious categories, such as leaving my camera on extreme settings and failing to realise this until halfway through a shoot the following day, or neglecting to take into account a critical variable until reviewing my work in the hotel bar when it's all too late. Both of which can be passed over, quietly forgotten, or placed in the category of deliberate mistake.

The truth is that for most of us, most of the time, nothing ever goes disastrously wrong, and we should be thankful. This is one of the reasons why the helicopter 'internal combustion' story is just that: a story, to be recounted with good-natured self-effacement over a beer as the nightingales sing in nearby Berkeley Square. If Julius Caesar was right in thinking that experience is the teacher of all things, then perhaps from this day on expedition helicopters are safer than they once were, if only because, as Hunter ruefully pointed out over the remains of his pint, "I'm not doing that again."

23

Be sure to wear some flowers in your hair

As the world commemorates the 50th anniversary of the Summer of Love, we should prepare for a deluge of retrospectives shot on film cameras with none of today's digital wizardry. Things were oh so very different then...

It was fifty years ago today. *Sgt. Pepper's Lonely Hearts Club Band* was unassailable at the top of the UK album charts for 23 consecutive weeks. No-one else got a look in. The Beatles were the only band in Britain to have a number one album during what we now call the Summer of Love. For those wondering what is the significance of this historical social phenomenon: it was simply a time when the world's youth found its voice. It started in San Francisco with a bunch of hippies protesting against the Vietnam War, but it spread globally and with it came the rejection of consumerist values. People grew their hair long, took acid and in their search for inner peace turned to Eastern mysticism. The social movement was to be encapsulated in the famous line from The Mamas & The Papas song that advised: "If you're going to San Francisco, be sure to wear some flowers in your hair".

Half a century later, as photographers, we can be sure that the Summer of Love had a profound effect on our world. While during the preceding decades photography had been cautiously feeling its way along, trying to work out what role it had to play, by the mid-1960s it was setting the agenda, from Carnaby Street fashion to the iconic news *reportage* in *Time Life*. While Larry Burrows and Paul Schutzer were sending home harrowing dispatches of the war in Vietnam, David Bailey was shooting the Beatles and Terence Donovan was immortalising Twiggy. On 25th June 1967, Jim Marshall snapped Jimi Hendrix on stage at a free concert at the Panhandle. One of the greatest ever rock photographers, he went on to capture Hendrix at Woodstock, famously refusing to sell for $25,000 the Leica he used to get the shot. "I'm like a reporter," said Marshall, "only with a camera. If it's going well, I get so immersed in it that I become at one with the camera".

If the Summer of Love was a time of counter-cultural rebellion, psychedelia, transcendental meditation and the liberal arts, it was also a time of photography, ushered in by the meteoric rise of the magazine. And although the magazine may not be quite so dominant today, as it makes way for as-yet-unproven digital platforms, back in the day paper ruled. Anthony Howarth, one of the most prolific 'colour supplement' snappers of the decade, with dozens of front covers for the *Telegraph* Sunday magazine, *National Geographic* and *Paris Match* to his name, remembers how photographers were as much part of the action as the musicians and models they photographed. Back in the sixties, Howarth cut a striking figure on the

Soho scene in his black leather jacket, driving a shark-like Citroën DS. When I dropped in to see him in his hacienda in southern France, Howarth told me that the life of the photographer could be lucrative: "You got paid decent fees in those days, especially on American magazines".

When it comes to cameras, it's tempting to think that the people behind them were struggling with antediluvian technology. While it was true that in 1967 there was no such thing as the digital instrument with its autofocus, on-board metering and data storage cards, it was also the year that saw the launch of the extraordinarily successful Leica M4 35 mm film rangefinder that was to stay with us until 1986. It was the era of the Olympus Trip 35 that would go on to sell more than 10 million units, and it was when the Polaroid Automatic 250 instant camera put in its first appearance. In many ways, we can look back on the sixties as the technological bridge connecting the more static classical world of plate photography – when the art form was in the hands of a cultural elite – to today's democratised digital frontier, where pretty much everyone with a smartphone thinks they're a photographer.

The output was phenomenal. While so few of the factual details of these events will stick in the mind, the photographs that make up the cultural record have become part of the fabric of the history of a world in flux. Curiously, some of the best-known protest photographs seem to have taken on a life of their own, where the image has acquired more significance than just a pictorial record of the act of rebellion. Bernie Boston's photographs of protesters offering flowers to military police at the Pentagon (there were several on the same theme) had an influential effect on the anti-war movement and are without doubt some of the most important examples of how photojournalism can be a force for good. Today, they are at the centre of academic debate about how graphic symbolism, such as that of the Flower Power movement (as well as the Nazi appropriation of the swastika), can have far-reaching social effects. The reason we remember the slogan 'Get the Hell out of Vietnam' is not because an academic or underground novelist wrote it, but because an anonymous student painted it on a placard to be captured on film for the world to see.

As the inevitable retrospectives celebrating flower power, civil rights, psychedelia and the mobilisation of the Baby Boomer generation start to open their doors to the public, it's probably worth reflecting on the notion that without the iconic photography (okay, and the music too), the Summer of Love would probably be little more than a few rarely read words on paper, a footnote to an era when the Cold War, Apollo missions and the Vietnam War were hogging the headlines.

24

Analogue *versus* digital...
This time it's personal

Revisiting the analogue versus digital debate doesn't get us any closer to understanding why sometimes we simply prefer one medium over another. It's easy to get lured into thinking digital is good while analogue is bad.

A few weeks ago, I was phoned by the commissioning editor of a highly respected technology magazine, who wanted me to put together a 'definitive' feature article comparing the virtues and faults of analogue film and digital sensors. My initial reaction was to politely decline on the basis that I know a poisoned chalice when I see one, for it should go without saying that whenever you claim to make a definitive statement about anything, someone who knows more about it will leap out of the woodwork and blow your argument to pieces, and I wasn't going anywhere near that sort of thing again. But the editor was persistent, informing me that it was high time we told the readers which was better, analogue or digital. "Aha," I said. "You didn't tell me you wanted me to come up with a value judgement."

That was I path I was not prepared to travel, came my reply. But I would, I reluctantly agreed, round up current expert opinion, while examining unambiguous objective data related to parameters such as resolution, dynamic range, light sensitivity. It won't come as that much of a surprise that in my resulting league tables, the digital sensor outperformed analogue film, often significantly.

Note that I use the colourless engineering term 'outperformed' rather than making any statement containing the subjective comparative 'better'. The reason for this is that photography is about so much more than megapixels and ISO 12232:2006 which, for the record, specifies "the method for assigning and reporting ISO speed ratings, ISO speed latitude ratings, standard output sensitivity values, and recommended exposure index values, for digital still cameras."

Which is why there are plenty of photographers out there who still use film, enjoy it, and as I found out recently, feel a spiritual call to do so. This I was told by a fine art photographer friend, who described how for her film has a 'warmth and humanity' that took her closer to what she was trying to articulate creatively than the sterility of the silicon chip. Not only that, the next generation of young photographers that she teaches in an American university thought so too. Although I could feel my cynicism for such statements mounting, I kept it under wraps, mostly because I was curious as to where her argument would lead.

The nuts and bolts of what followed was that she essentially believed there to be mystic voodoo in analogue technology that doesn't exist in the digital realm. And although I think this borders on nonsense, the choice to use film for whatever reason is a personal one, and I cannot find it in myself to accuse her of being wrong. After all, we're all guilty of wanting a little 'sympathetic magic' in our lives. Otherwise, why would we ask authors to sign first editions of their hardback novels, when we can download, for a fraction of the price, the identical text onto our e-readers? Because, traditional paper along with a few handwritten words takes us deeper – albeit irrationally – into that author's world.

I remained unconvinced. After all, the substrate on which we capture our photons is conspicuously on the technical end of what we do, no matter how creative the result might be. The data doesn't lie, and digital files contain more information than film. Fact. Put it this way, with a few clicks of the mouse and a film emulation software programme, I can make a digital photograph look as though it came out of a plate camera a century ago, assuming I'd ever wish to. With fairly rudimentary digital technology, I can scan, repair and restore old analogue prints and preserve them for all eternity in a virtual and limitless world. Film? Not so much.

On the other hand... not my words, but those of digital guru and Prefab Sprout producer Thomas Dolby. As improbable as it sounds, we were having a spot of luncheon in the metropolis the other day, during which I found myself recounting the conversation with my fine art film photographer friend, expecting the man who ushered in the world of digital audio technology to have some alignment with my views on the dubious nature of sympathetic magic as an artistic process. He was, after all, one of the pioneers of the Fairlight audio workstation that revolutionised the digital soundscape. Surely, he would agree with me.

"On the other hand," Dolby repeated, visibly unwilling to come down on either side of the argument, "things take longer in the analogue space." He went on to explain that when he'd felt restricted creatively by immature technology in the past, he had been forced to experiment and, due to these experiments having a tendency to be long, tedious and unsuccessful, he'd found himself having to think things through carefully beforehand. Now with digital, he elaborated, because everything can be done quickly, you can fiddle about to your heart's content, using trial and error as a problem-solving technique in a non-destructive editing environment. It followed therefore that artistic creation using a more primitive form of technology could potentially produce a deeper level of engagement. In which case, he elaborated, film might well indeed take some photographers closer to the mind of God than their smartphones ever could. In a blinding flash I saw why Dolby is seen as a genius in his world.

Keen to salvage something from my theory that rational objectivity inevitably trumps irrational subjectivity, as we stepped out onto the street I made one final attempt to defend myself. "But you will at least accept that the message is the message and the medium is the medium?"

Dolby looked at me as if to say "If you say so", before disappearing into the back streets of London.

25

The perils and pleasures of photographic planning

When it comes to planning expeditions, some of us will be conscientious, while others will be impulsive. But the question is, which of these approaches yields better pictures? No need to decide. We're all different.

Of human nature much can be learned by listening to our fellow photographers. Having interviewed more than a hundred during the past decade I've started to realise what ideas unite us. I have come to know when and why we find ourselves waving to each other across a chasm of differing opinion. Within our vast congregation of 'people with cameras' there are clearly defined outlooks, along with less lucid, fuzzier sets of data that would combine to make a complex and intriguing Venn diagram.

Were that graphic to be coloured in, no doubt it would be very pretty, but I suspect it wouldn't reveal anything further in the way of a definitive statement about the 'right' way to do things. Looking deeper into the diagram's complexities reveals that one of the areas of most robust division is that of photographic planning. I'm not talking about the type of preparation that is sometimes called 'previsualisation', in which a specific composition already exists in the 'mind's eye' of the photographer, and where all that remains is to go out and hunt it down. Rather, I have in mind the type of forethought that dictates whither our photographic muse will lead us as we stand at the threshold of our front door at dawn, deciding whether to venture forth to the left or right, on foot or by bicycle, on the train or by car.

It won't come as much of a surprise to discover that, on the basis of my – admittedly unscientific – conclusions drawn from conversations with some of the best photographers working today, we're pretty much split down the middle and happily so. Half of us, it would appear, are content to trust to fortune when we step into the great outdoors, while the other half will have spent much of the previous night immersed in OS maps, GPS co-ordinates, tide and train timetables. You won't find me pronouncing in favour of either. But I do think that both are capable of producing tremendous results, while simultaneously being equally vulnerable to failure. It all comes down to personal choice. Or does it?

Anyone who has ever attended one of those tedious business seminars that claim to turn you into a Bransonesque entrepreneur will be familiar with the character of the snake-oil salesman in the form of a 'management guru' drilling into their audience the '5 Ps': 'Proper Planning Prevents Poor Performance'. I'm not sure if these are same management gurus as those telling us with the same grinning self-assurance the exact opposite, in that there are 'five ways to improvise your way to success'. But these ridiculous examples serve to prove what we as photographers have known since the beginning of time, which is that for some of us spontaneity and the ability to react quickly will produce better photos, while for others the surest route to success is a measured, structured and analytical approach. While some fear to take so much as a single step off the path, there will be others saying, "What path? I didn't even know there was one." And this is because there is something innate about what we do as photographers. We might use roughly speaking the same instrumentation, and we might have roughly speaking the same goals, but there is an astonishing breadth of interpretation as to how we put them to use... roughly speaking.

Most of us, I suspect, fall somewhere between the two extremes of the spectrum. While I have interviewed plenty of photographers who genuinely wish that they could be more flexible, there have been as many who feel that the injection of even a smidgen of discipline into their world would work wonders. If we are truly on a journey of what our management consultants call, in their ghastly language of business communication, 'continuous improvement' then it's hardly surprising that from time to time we might seek to emulate those we perceive to be achieving better results.

Some time ago I was commissioned to take a portrait of the distinguished travel writer and novelist Colin Thubron. While I composed my shot of the author (who's no mean photographer in his own right), I took it on myself to ask him all those irritating questions that writers hate being distracted by. Before long we'd settled on the very same debate, discussing the pleasures and the perils of planning our creative output. It was a subject close to his heart and his views seemed to point to a reasonable compromise between spontaneity and calculation. The bones of what he told me was that while he was happy to write his novels to a plan, his travelogues were fundamentally more improvised in design. How you approach your art depends on what you want to achieve. Thubron, it seems, uses both strategies.

But you've got to know which one works better. There was a time, he told me, when he tailored his journeys according to a concept drawn up in advance. But this was frustrating, because it seemed to drain the meaning out of the experience. Often, he'd find himself rebelling against the plan, deviating from the itinerary simply because he was fed up with it and wanted to improvise, to take a look down that road over there, precisely because what lay at the other end was unknown. Other times, the horse would go lame, the bus would break down or a Kalashnikov-toting, vodka-swigging border guard would threaten to shoot you. These were the real experiences, said Thubron, and if you thought you could write a plan for that, you were deceiving yourself.

26

When post-pro takes us down the garden path

*There was a time when post-production was no more
complex than opening a cardboard envelope full of newly
developed transparencies. But today, the process of
digital post-pro seems to be replacing photography itself.*

Decades ago, when I did my long-haired stint in the
professional audio business or the 'music industry' as it
was sometimes informally called, I witnessed a polar
cultural shift in the way musicians used recording studios
and their attitude towards the recording medium. As
studios made the transition from the analogue sound wave
to digital, the purpose of the studio – especially in the
consumer world of mainstream rock – began to change.
While studio recordings were once seen merely as
reminders of live performances (as they often still are in
the classical space), live performances mutated into
becoming reminders of the records we had left at home.

Artists replaced live spontaneity with agonisingly dull replications of what they had often painstakingly created in the artificial world of the studio.

There's something similar going on in the world of photography at the moment. I've recently taken to walking in the countryside and along the coast of my native Wales without a camera. This is a deliberate ploy, designed to help me reach a better understanding of what photographs I actually want to take. I find that being without my camera focuses the mind in the way shooting on film once did. Of course, the process is self-defeating because it is hard to take photographs without a camera. And yet, as I walk something gnaws away in the grey matter, and it is this. Increasingly the actual landscapes I see before me are starting to remind me of photographs, rather than the photographs I see reminding me of landscapes. And although I can't quite put my finger on why this seems to be an inversion of the natural order of things, I instinctively know that it is.

This is because I think photography is in a phase of convergence. Here at the dawn of the Golden Age of digital it may sound counterintuitive, but it is an observable fact that mainstream photography is rushing to the safe ground, and is becoming defined by a handful of creative diktats that are fast becoming parodies of themselves. Who do I blame for this convergence? Not the photographer, that's as sure as mustard. But we must share some of the fault in refusing to challenge a risk-averse society choking on its own traumatised liberal anxiety. It is the overwhelming need to not be wrong that stops the media in particular from doing things right. That's what drives advertising creatives, coffee table book editors and competition organisers to the pictorial safe ground. The worst irony of living in an era in which we daily remind ourselves of our commitment to diversity is that we, of course, are becoming more clone-like by the second, regurgitating a dubious orthodoxy as if it were holy writ. Today, it seems everything must be the same in order to survive. This is never truer than in photography.

And the key weapon in this mind control? Well, it would be easy to lay the blame at the door of those photo-sharing platforms that create a meaningless ubiquity to snapshot photography. But I think that's outside the argument. The real culprit is the power of post-production editing software. Here we have at our fingertips the potential to make any photograph look like anything we want, and yet we waste that power in the pursuit of applying layer after layer of special effects that ultimately make our photographs bear little resemblance to anything other than other people's photographs. Once upon a time post-processing was no more complex than opening a cardboard sleeve to see in what state the transparencies had come back from the developer. Now, we spend our lives rebuilding images pixel by pixel in an attempt to make them look identical to everyone else's.

If this sounds as though I'm paraphrasing the dystopia of *Nineteen Eighty-Four*, I should point out that I am deliberately exaggerating and playing devil's advocate to make my case. And yet, the reason we can't produce the diversity of work that we once did is because we are hamstrung by a pervading dogma that leads us up the garden path. We have become too comfortable with the centrist ideal of 'not upsetting the horses' and in doing so have lost our ability to stick two fingers up to the world and say, "sorry buddy, but I'm doing it my way." On the other hand, if it is your ambition to be published in the mainstream, win competitions and produce monographs, the world is your oyster and Elysian Fields all rolled into one. There's not much wrong with that and there's never been a better time to do it. It's just not very exciting.

It seems to me that there are two conventional but opposing conclusions to be drawn here. To the 'glass half full' chap there is the consolation that at least the bar is being raised and that the overall quality of our work is getting better. If in the process it becomes homogenised then that is the cost of doing business, besides which, this homogeneity is one of the characteristics of the *zeitgeist*. Part of the evolution of photography, if you like.

Meanwhile, the 'glass half empty' chap will detect a slight feeling of doom in the pit of the stomach that says the price we pay for increased quality is a bafflingly unnecessary convergence, despite having ever better tools with which to diverge. I'm not sure that I'm very attracted to either of these ideas. I suspect, as I have done ever since the solid-state digital audio recording machine replaced the analogue reel-to-reel tape recorder, that the glass is twice as big as it need be.

27

An ill wind that blew
nobody any good

*Recent hurricanes in the Gulf of Mexico have caused
untold destruction from which it will take years to
recover. I was due out there on assignment, but luckily
got turned back en route to Heathrow.*

It was on a pleasantly sunny morning last September, as I
was threading my way to Heathrow Airport on the
London Underground, when I thought to scan my mobile
phone one last time for any messages before putting
myself through the pre-boarding meat-grinder that is
check in. As I was on my way to South Carolina to visit
the Low Country on a travel shoot for a fancy London
style magazine, I wasn't really expecting anything too
dramatic. Maybe a deadline or two brought forward, or a
few queries about some missing hi-res files. It had never
even crossed my mind that an entire trip could be
cancelled at the drop of a hat. But it had been.

There on my screen was an email from my American hosts saying that not only should I not take the flight across the Pond but, as there was an evacuation warning due to the projected arrival of Hurricane Irma over the next few days, they were nervous about how they'd get me back to Blighty. Most of the major airlines were already starting to wind down operations on the south-eastern seaboard, while those that were still hanging in there were cancelling schedules left, right and centre. What return flights remained were spiralling into a frenzy of dynamic pricing that meant, even if I could book a seat on my proposed return journey, I'd probably only get as far as another hub such as New York, for which I could expect to pay upwards of ten thousand dollars.

Rolling along on the Piccadilly line, my immediate thought was that this was one of those thoroughly modern over-reactions you get these days. But on checking with my hosts, I was quickly brought to the opinion that they were deadly serious and sorry for the inconvenience. But there was also a tacit level of between-the-lines anxiety that seemed to say that they had enough on their plates without being responsible for the well-being of a British photographer who was still safely on the other side of the Atlantic. Somewhat bemused, I did the only rational thing I could, which was to get off the train – I think at Boston Manor – and retrace my steps, rueing that I'd cleared out my diary, postponed other assignments and was staring into a hole in my schedule that would inevitably lead to a corresponding aperture in my end-of-year accounts.

Of course, I was grateful to my American contacts for putting my safety ahead of other considerations. The weather forecast, they told me, was such that even if Irma didn't rip South Carolina apart over the next few days, the conditions were unlikely to be conducive to the sort of sumptuous magazine photography we were hoping for, and there was no alternative but to scratch the fixture. Over the following days I tracked Irma's progress northwest through the Caribbean and watched as the tail of the weather system beat its way up to South Carolina. I was later told that the exact region I was to be photographing had taken a battering and, while being nowhere near as bad as that on the Caribbean islands, the destruction to the hotel I was booked into was serious enough. No one had been injured, but it was now without a roof, while the level of chaos, even at this relatively low level of impact, had to be seen to be believed.

We can probably agree that as near-death experiences go, mine wasn't very near at all. But it did get me reflecting on the precarious nature of life on the road as a freelance photographer. Of course, the inconvenience I underwent was as nothing compared with the effect that Irma had on the people of the Caribbean and in no way am I attempting to put my setbacks on the same level as those left without loved ones, homes or jobs. But even at this distant end of the scale, I could see the far-reaching effects of such a natural disaster rippling out into the distant waters. I thanked my lucky stars that those very same stars had aligned themselves in such a way as to keep me well clear of the central tragedy.

Of course, what people feel in situations similar to this is what psychologists term 'survivor guilt': a phenomenon that prevents us from rationally accepting our good fortune and moving on with our lives. But this is what you have to do, because if you just sit there thinking 'it could have been me,' you will run the risk of drawing the confused conclusion that while the impact on the self is negligible compared with others, its significance is not. You preface every statement with self-indulgent whimsy along the lines of 'there but for the grace of God go I', while secretly and guiltily thinking that you've dodged a bullet. I remember when a fashion photographer friend got caught up in the 9/11 terror attack in New York. For months after the event he thought the entire disaster was his own fault and that in surviving the atrocity he'd somehow betrayed those that had perished.

As we now enter the calm after the storm and the Gulf of Mexico enters a phase of reconstruction, my plucky friends, as they now are, have repaired their hotel and reissued my invitation to photograph it soon. I'll let you know how I get on.

28

A lesson from the top
of the mountain

It is an incontestable truth that the tools of our trade are frighteningly expensive. Not even the richest of us can afford to brush off the careless loss of so much as lens cap. We owe it to ourselves to be vigilant with our gear...

One of the best nuggets of non-photographic wisdom I ever learned about photography came to me at the top of a mountain in Africa. It wasn't, as you might suppose, a moment of existential enlightenment handed down by a tribal elder, and it certainly didn't come from above. As I trudged back down the mountain, neither did I feel the triumph of Moses returning from the heights of Sinai with his tablets of stone. But it was nonetheless something of reverential import that I have chosen never to forget. As the sun set over the apricot-coloured expanse of the Hartmann's Valley, Josh said to me in hushed tones, "You've got to respect your gear, man. It's easy to lose."

I was a young togger then, on one of my first magazine assignments. My travelling companion was a vastly more experienced photographer in the travel genre, winner of competitions and published by the likes of *National Geographic*. Although I probably got on his nerves with my incessant questions – principal among which was "What are you doing now and why?" – Josh was a patient teacher, keen to impart his hard-won knowledge of what made the world of the jobbing photographer go around. "Losses and breakages eat into your fee. You must extend the life of everything in your kit to preserve your operating margins. The very last thing you want is to waste money on replacing gear you already own."

As darkness fell, we descended the mountain sure-footed and wiser. Because it was only a small mountain with a well-worn track over easy ground, and because we could see the twinkling lights of our camp at Palmwag, we made it home without incident and in plenty of time to slosh down a few pre-dinner G&Ts. As we reviewed our day's catch on the backs of our cameras, Josh let out a muted howl of irritation. "Damn and blast," he ejaculated with a dramatic intensity more usually reserved for the Globe theatre. "I left my lens cap on top of the mountain."

Quickly sensing how irksome it can be for the pupil to draw attention to the failings of the master, especially in a situation so heavily charged with poetic irony, and doubly especially after the urgent sincerity of his Sermon on the Mount, I confined myself to nodding sympathetically. "Oh well," said Josh. "Nothing for it. We'll have to go back up there and get it." While the expression "are you serious?" was welling up in my interior 'what to say next' queue, I could see that never had a man been more in earnest, an attitude confirmed with the words: "You said you wanted to learn about photography. Welcome to one of the harder lessons." And so unable to come up with any reasonable objection to his plan beyond simply not wanting to, I set my alarm for 04:00, put the matter out of my mind and went about the evening's entertainment, which consisted mainly of poring over maps and GPS units, while discussing our route over the salt-pale gypsum plains of the Namib desert for the following day.

Dawn broke roughly speaking two hours after we'd left camp and only a moment or two before we reached the summit of our small mountain for the second time in twenty-four hours. While I'd been harbouring doubts that we'd ever see Josh's lens cap again in this world, much to my surprise it was exactly where he had said it would be. He picked it up with a degree of satisfaction that didn't seem to sit too well with the fact that the entire enterprise was down to his carelessness in the first place. And yet, the opportunity to grab a few sunrise shots was too good to miss. By the time we had trudged back down the track, our guide was busily honking the horn of the Land Rover at the trailhead in the valley, swearing robustly in Afrikaans and with a face like a bulldog chewing a wasp.

After several hours of rolling along parallel to a dry river bed in the scorching African sun, I summoned up the courage to express my opinion to Josh that while we'd been lucky to get out of Palmwag with our photographic inventory intact, perhaps the effort of climbing the mountain once more had been disproportionate to our goal: namely the retrieval of a measly lens cap.

That would depend on how you look at these things, replied Josh, before embarking on a lengthy declamation on the nature of the intrinsic value of the tools of the trade, that on reflection amounted to little more than 'if you look after your gear then your gear will look after you.' Despite not being even remotely tempted by the notion of karma, and despite at the time thinking that he was doing little more than covering up his embarrassment with homespun truisms, years later I can see that he had a point of sorts. If you have ever mislaid a twenty-pound note and spent the best part of an hour fruitlessly looking for it – which I assume includes every one of us – you will see it too.

The fact of the matter is that the kit we have in our gadget bags has taken time and money to accrue. We can't help natural wear and tear, and only the luckiest of us will get through their career without having their equipment stolen. But we can all take a leaf out of Josh's book and reduce our losses due to lack of vigilance.

29

Too quick to see
you later, alligator

*A chance to photograph alligators in America's Deep
South produces a perfect 'blink and you miss it' moment,
while capturing the 'Spirit of America' with a classic bald
eagle shot falls flat on the grounds of mistaken identity.*

With the tail of Hurricane Irma having blown its way
through South Carolina, and with all the fallen trees
hauled away and roofs returned to their buildings,
Palmetto Bluff was looking as pretty as a picture. I
couldn't have asked for better conditions in which to go
photographing. Just to remind you, I was on assignment
for one of those fashionable London magazines that has
travel pages, in which the photography serves a slightly
different function from that of a glossy fine art or
photographic magazine. I won't say it's not as important,
and I can assure you that I take it deadly seriously. But
travel commissions are a bit like picking strawberries in

that you select the juiciest, sweetest ones as quickly as you can and head for the weigh-in station happy to have finished. You're neither expected nor required to produce anything improvised or original, and no one will thank you for submitting images not on the 'shot list' (no matter how creatively innovative they might be). The result of which is that your downtime tends to be your own. Since I'd never been to the Low Country or shot alligators before, I decided that this would be the order of the day.

One of the first things you'll hear in South Carolina is that alligators aren't crocodiles. They enjoy a much more serene reputation for being calm and reasonable, quite unlike their larger, more aggressive cousins. They are protected by conservation laws to a level that borders on mollycoddling and they certainly won't attack you unless you do something really stupid, like try to feed them. They can be a nuisance in that they can't be relocated, and are indifferent to the convenience of human beings in their choice of places to sunbathe. But, by and large, they are a harmless variety of crocodilian that, to employ the cliché, are more afraid of you than you are of them.

And so it was with something of a song in my heart that I mounted the pushbike and headed down to a sleepy creek where, I had been assured, there were plenty of alligators to be found. Not only that, there was an *olde worlde* wooden bridge spanning some picturesque sandbars with a wonderful backdrop of Carolinian swamp positively teeming with great blue heron and snowy egret.

As I unpacked my camera, apart from the sun making its stately transit across the Empyrean sphere and a few bald eagles spiralling on steep thermals, nothing moved. It was as if the world had gone to sleep. There wasn't a breath of wind and I could feel the suspension of leaves on their branches. Here was peace like no other I had ever experienced. Luckily for me there was a pair of alligators

126

already warming up within range of my lens, and so all I needed was to wait for something to happen. And so, I waited. And waited. And waited. Now I know that a lot of people dislike waiting for even the kettle to boil, but I was brought up with a fishing rod in my hand. Patience comes naturally to me and the apparently motionless passing of time holds no fear for me either.

But as the sun rose, my face reddened and my throat became parched, I came to realise that one of the things that the good people of South Carolina had failed to mention is that alligators don't move so much as an eyelid muscle for hours on end. After what seemed like an eternity, I decided to stretch my legs. Ambling across the bridge, I heard from behind me a silky splash as both alligators slid into the water. My one chance for gator action this day had gone, it seemed.

As I cycled back the handful of miles to Palmetto Bluff in the early evening, I noticed ahead of me half a dozen bald eagles soaring in the golden air. Deciding that I'd never seen anything quite so quintessentially *American* in my life, I dismounted and walked along a riverbank, eyes and camera pointing upward. And although I didn't *quite* tread on the fully-grown alligator asleep in the long grass before me, I was brought up pretty sharpish only a few feet from a head-on collision.

Now, at moments like this you forget all the rational data about how safe they are, and all you can think of is that this might be the alligator that wants revenge for all those handbags, belts and shoes. I can't say the sins of my past flashed before my eyes, but I can report that I didn't know what to do, and so in the absence of a better plan, did nothing. My riverine friend eyed me with suspicion, evidently unwilling to call the first shot. Then of all the bizarre things you can imagine, I saw an old man out walking his dog.

"Good day, sir," I hallooed, not forgetting my recently acquired Southern politeness, before asking him what advice he had for getting me out of the predicament I was in. "Sir, you need to step away from the alligator," quoth the man with a certain amount of logic, before adding: "I don't think it will bite you." Later as we talked, and while I took some rather handsome portraits of the 13-footer, my new friend told me that there have been only eight alligator attacks in South Carolina in the past half century, and all of those had happened only after the humans in question had, predictably, tried to feed them.

"And by the way, sir," he said as we shook hands: "they ain't eagles. They're fish hawks. Everyone makes that mistake."

30

The ghost in the
photographic machine?

There will come a day when our gear must fall apart.
But when all my equipment started to disintegrate at once,
I was left wondering whether there was something a tad
more sinister going on than everyday wear and tear...

I'm not much of an enthusiast for those tedious
homespun axioms by Murphy, Finagle or Sod. But as
widgets and grommets went walkabout, zips got fatally
jammed, connectors refused to connect, editing software
expired, data card capacity mysteriously shrank and
walking boots started to leak, I did begin to think that
there might at least be a ghost in the machine. To crown it
all – and this was when I came to concur with the Bard
when he spoke of the whirligig of time bringing in his
revenges – I was plagued by that most niggling of minor
torments caused by the fact that my camera's inlay fascia
for the rotary control that selects functions such as

aperture or shutter priority was now marked absent. How can you, I wondered aloud, shell out the hard-earned to the tune of thousands of pounds, only to fall at the first fence due to a design flaw as basic as this?

Necessity being the mother of invention, I combed through my irritatingly large stock of retired camera bodies to see if something could be filched from one and jury-rigged to the other. But, with no two such dials being the same, the enterprise was a complete waste of time; a commodity I was obliged to waste even more of as I dug around in my camera's software working out how to display what was once a perfectly straightforward manually controlled function on its screen. All of which put me in a foul mood that led my thoughts to a design phenomenon that, while sounding like an urban myth or conspiracy theory, is to the technology ecosystem what oxygen and carbon are to biology.

Planned obsolescence comes in two basic forms. The first happens when new models in the design cycle are launched with such high frequency that they deliberately render perfectly functional products old-fashioned. As photographers we might sometimes find ourselves alarmed by the fact that our relatively new camera body is already out of date. In the manufacturers' defence this can also be attributed to Moore's Law, which basically says that the number of transistors you can cram on a chip will double every two years. Since no-one's going to halve the price of their cameras, in a world dominated by silicon, the instruments will just acquire more bells and whistles to justify the expense and extra computing power.

The knock-on effect is that we are bombarded with more new models hitting the market with greater frequency, compelling the consumer to take the so-called 'opportunity' or be sadly left behind. Personally, I've given up worrying what anyone thinks when I turn up to a shoot with a DSLR that's two years (and so one entire generation of Moore's Law) out of date.

The second form of built-in obsolescence is harder to understand in that some products are deliberately built to stop working after a certain period of time, creating the necessity (rather than opportunity) for the consumer to spend more money on a replacement. It's as much an economic balancing act as it is taking a punt on your customers' attitudes. But if market research shows that we don't mind replacing, say, our washing machines after seven years, what would be the point in designing them to last for a decade? And although this won't necessarily apply in the fast-moving world of camera design where there is occasionally a certain amount of innovation, manufacturers still cosmetically restyle their product – as the American car maker Chevrolet did in the 1920s – in the hope that these annual facelifts will disguise the fact that they're flogging old technology.

Talking of cars, years ago when journalists were routinely supplied with one by their employer, I used to drive around London (it was before the Congestion Charge, too) in a brand spanking new 2-litre Vauxhall Cavalier. Those were the days and weirdly there was nothing unusual in that. However, an editor friend of mine, deciding that he was perfectly happy with his 27-year-old Ford Anglia, denied himself the option of a swanky new automobile and opted for a cash equivalent instead. All was going swimmingly well until a photographic assignment took him to Ford's manufactory in Dagenham or somewhere like that. As he pulled into the visitors' car park an energetic marketing executive appeared from nowhere and greeted him with words to the effect that he should park that heap of junk elsewhere.

"Heap of junk?" retorted the aback-taken editor, who had assumed that the car manufacturer would have been only too pleased to be reacquainted with an old friend. "We only want new cars in the car park," explained the marketing executive sniffily, who without explicitly saying so, strongly implied that the appearance of an antediluvian incarnation of his company's product was an embarrassment not just because it was ancient, but because it hadn't fallen apart as planned.

Technology isn't supposed to last for ever and, as with the case of the Ford Anglia, in those rare exceptions when it does, there are distinctly mixed feelings all round. There was a time when we didn't seem to mind hand-me-down cameras, and yet these days it seems so old fashioned. I talk to photographers from the pre-digital age that recall with genuine affection how their father bequeathed to them his old 35 mm film SLR or evergreen medium format TLR. But I can hardly envisage a future in which their digital counterparts will be passed along the successive generations with quite such ceremony.

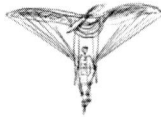

31

When increased reputation is the real prize

As a bizarre series of events conspired to make what should have been a moment of professional pride feel more like a snub, I discovered that winning competitions isn't always what it's cracked up to be.

You won't often find me writing on camera technology at design or manufacture level. But when I do it tends to be for an international engineering magazine based in the UK that I've contributed to for donkey's years. This was the same engineering magazine that, unbeknownst to me, recently entered my feature article on vintage analogue photographic equipment for a journalism award. Imagine my reaction when, completely out of the blue I discovered a communiqué in my electronical mail inbox alerting me to the fact that I had the glory of winning a competition I'd never heard of, and was now entitled to style myself the *International something-or-other Writer of the Year*.

Speaking as a professional who would rather be paid actual money than be patted on the head like a small child, I maintained a studied indifference to the accolade. You'll forgive me if I can't quite remember the award's name in full, because it was at this point everything descended into a quagmire of corporate doublespeak disguising a petty snub. A subsequent email informed me with all the largesse of Lady Bountiful that should I wish to fly to attend the awards dinner in the United States of America, I was perfectly entitled to do so provided it was at my own expense. However, the email continued, should I avail myself of this contingency, it should be after clearly understanding the publisher's policy in such matters stating that physical trophies won by freelancers on behalf of the company remained the property of the company, which then may or may not be exhibited in the company's trophy cabinet at their head office.

Faced with the prospect of funding an intercontinental mission to collect a worthless gewgaw that legally belonged to someone else and that had been won in a competition that I hadn't even been aware of entering, I adopted the time-honoured journalistic protocol of making my excuses and leaving, if not physically then mentally. The cynic might be tempted to summarise that the sum total of what I received that glorious day was an email stuffed with pretty much nothing other than ill-will. The publisher might as well have opted simply not to tell me that I had won the award in the first place. But as that had no cruelty in it, neither had it any sport.

I've written many times on my conflicting and changing opinions about photography competitions. I have also written on what I consider to be reasonable tactics to adopt in order to boost your chances of winning them and how to second-guess what the judges are looking for. I've even, in a moment of hot-headedness that I now partially regret, dismissed the photography competition altogether, once claiming that 'competitions are for horses' and therefore have no place in the world of serious photography. But having been forced to confront the surreal ignominy of the ordeal I have described above; I find myself in an oddly positive frame of mind about such contests. I have come to see that underneath all this grey-suited middle management jobsworthiness I had actually won something that went beyond the traditional and trashy engraved Perspex ornament.

I had reached an understanding of what it means for the winner to win, an understanding of the checks and balances brought to the world of photography by the occasional arm-wrestle with a panel of judges. You could go even further and suggest that perhaps the competition is something of a health check by which we assess the strength of the pulse of the body corporate. Ultimately, I reasoned, whether I flew to the States dressed in a penguin suit to pick up a gong was somehow of less importance than the idea that the article had impressed the judges sufficiently to place it first in the race. It meant that I could stake my claim to have earned ranking among some serious names. I felt that despite being rudely cheated of glory, I'd significantly gained in professional reputation, a concept about which I am usually suspicious.

As ungrateful as I may sound – I really would have quite liked a brown envelope stuffed with cash to go with my increased reputation – the real prize is simply that of recognition before your peers and it is worth more than mere money. While I will stick to my guns and say that I can't imagine a world in which you could ever objectively win a photography competition (in the way that you can win a horse race), I will say that I am moved to the opinion that 'success' in such enterprises propels you into a network that will get you noticed.

Without a reputation for being good at what you do, it's difficult to find work or get published. We all know of brilliant reclusive photographers who never show their work to anyone because they're more interested in the act of artistic creation than accruing the benefits of recognition. But such people are few and far between, and even prone to change their minds. We would do well to remember the poet Dante Gabriel Rossetti who, having buried a sheaf of unpublished poems with his dead wife, later exhumed her remains to retrieve his manuscripts. Rosetti, it seems, was more unwilling to face the future without his poetry being published than without his wife.

This may have been an extraordinary act of vanity, but it was vanity derived from the assumption that it is better for your work to be seen by the fee-paying public than to remain unseen. For us photographers, whether we like it or not, the competition is unfortunately one of the most efficient ways of making that happen.

32

A way of putting it,
not very satisfactory

We all want to take better photos, and we want to 'raise the bar'. But should we really be borrowing clichés from the world of sport, when there is ample opportunity to push the boat out and come up with some of our own?

It would be a supremely accomplished or sadly deluded photographer that thought there was no longer any room for improvement in their creative output. In either case that photographer would be an extremely rare and possibly endangered species, and I have yet to meet one. No one, it would seem, is sufficiently daft or vain to say aloud that the top of the game has been reached and all that remains is to rest on the photographic laurels. In fact, one of the most common themes to spontaneously emerge in interviews I conduct with photographers is the need for what is sometimes called in the world of high-tech manufacturing 'continuous improvement'.

You could argue that 'CI' (as it has been dubbed by modern management aficionados) is such an obvious feature of the human condition that it hardly needs a special name. But special name it has, deriving ultimately from the Japanese concept of *kaizen* (where 'kai' means 'change' and 'zen' means 'good').

We all want to become better photographers, and it is interesting that nearly everyone who makes this point puts it in terms of 'raising the bar'. It is an image taken from field sports, such as pole vaulting or the high jump, to imply that if a task is made incrementally more difficult then we will strive for and attain higher goals. There is nothing wrong with that, apart from it being a curiously negative metaphor to apply to photography. This is because even the winners are losers in one sense, as it is rare that they will accept victory without having 'one more go', which by the defining parameters of the sport means that the end is only the end when the bar has crashed to the ground for the last time. It may only be a small point, and it may just be a function of our routinely using sports imagery carelessly, but to define success in terms of failure is somewhat out of alignment with photography's creative spirit.

If we accept that it stands to reason that we all want to get better, perhaps a more evolved approach might be to ask how we go about doing this. If we take it as axiomatic that there is always room for improvement then it follows that all we have to do is listen to how other photographers got better, collate the data and create a system. I have interviewed hundreds of award-winning editorial or commercial photographers working in every field from landscape to wildlife, astrophotography to portraiture, lensless to remote-operated drones. After casting out the wackier of the outliers, within the distribution curve there are five clearly defined approaches to progress. If this were one of those annoying flip-chart demonstrations I would give each an initial letter and come up with a catchy acronym. But since this isn't business school, and because my acronym is the decidedly flimsy TIERS (well, it could have been the even weaker RITES or the downright patronising TRIES), I'll get on with what's important and leave the task of working out how to remember five words to you.

First, we have *time*. Nearly everyone agrees that we don't devote enough of this rare commodity to getting to know our equipment and putting it into action. Second, we have *influence*, which is the need to review the work of others, perhaps by sitting down with a monograph by Ansel Adams or Henri Cartier-Bresson, trying to understand what makes their photographs better than ours. Influence could equally extend to mugging up on technique in a magazine or going down the pub with a fellow photographer. We don't do enough of this, especially the latter. Then we have *experimentation*, represented by the central letter of the acronym and central to all development. This could be in the form of something as basic as investigating what those weird buttons that you never use actually do, to thinking about some of the established rules of conventional photography and working out ways to break them.

We get a subtle double next in the form of *repetition* and *repeatability*, where the former specifically refers to revisiting locations and subject matter in order to gain deeper insight, while the latter is all about being able to replicate image quality, especially under pressure. It's not much use to anyone if you become adept at getting all your critical variables spot on in rehearsal, only to get stage fright when you've got to make the image stick. We could call this practice, but the word isn't big enough. You've just got to keep doing it until, to paraphrase

George Orwell, habit becomes instinct. Finally, we arrive at *self-evaluation*. We all know when our work has passed the quality inspection and when it hasn't: we must be ruthless in our judgement. We have to be sure to take an unsentimental approach to what ends up on the cutting room floor.

Despite the temptation to do so, there is nothing to be gained from arranging these points into a hierarchy, as they are fundamentally joined together in the way that the geometrical pentagram is formed. If you follow the line around, you will pass through every single node in a continuous journey, because each is directly or indirectly linked to every other (mediaeval English literature aficionados will at this point wish to point me in the direction of the line from *Sir Gawain and the Green Knight*, in which Gawain's five knightly virtues were "uchone halched in other, that non ende hade").

So, having come up with something more useful, let's have no more talk about 'raising the bar'. It's far too small a concept to contain the subtleties involved with becoming a better photographer.

33

Becoming the best judge
of your best shot

While it's tempting to think that we are the best judges of our own work, even the most experienced photographer needs a helping hand. Not least because there could be something of worth in the archive that you'd never see.

There are plenty of compelling reasons to enjoy being a magazine editor, but the aspect of sitting in the Big Chair at *Geographical* I enjoyed most was when a photographer came to pitch me a new photo set. In fact, it was such a pleasant part of the job that I'd try to orchestrate my diary in such a way that the prospecting photographer took up my last appointment of the day, the idea being that should the meeting look like over-running there would be no pressure to wrap up or make hasty decisions. As I got to know my core group of regular photographers these sessions routinely spilled over into Soho's *Dog & Duck*.

Chief among my regulars was a brilliant and fearless snapper who I will call Bob. The pseudonym is required because I'm going to say something mildly critical of him and I don't want to hurt his feelings. As I say, Bob was a genius with the camera and all that went with it, often embracing what others would consider to be unacceptable risk in pursuit of his craft. He would inveigle his way behind the frontlines of conflict, into zones of natural disaster and right into the heart of humanitarian crises. He once told me that he'd fallen out of a helicopter in Iraq. But he'd been lucky, because despite breaking several bones, his cameras survived unscarred. So, you get the picture. I had, and still have, deep respect for Bob as both photographer and man.

All this, and yet whenever I got a call to meet him at the *Dog & Duck* to 'have a quick look' at his latest haul, my heart would sink a millimetre or two. This was because Bob would always bring thousands – and I mean literally thousands – of transparencies to our meetings in several enormous lever arch folders.

Although I took it in good humour, after a few such entanglements I decided to gently investigate whether Bob would be prepared to trim down the vastness of his presentations and perhaps leave me with two or three edited sets of more manageable proportions for my consideration. Things came to a head one hot sunny afternoon as up he bounded like an exuberant dog, overburdened by files and wearing a bulletproof vest. "What on earth are you wearing that for?" I asked not unreasonably. "Oh that," he replied. "Well, it was a bit cumbersome to carry, what with all these photos."

Delving deeper I discovered that he was using his trip to Town not just to see me, but also to procure body armour for a forthcoming assignment in either the Western Sahara or Sudan, I forget which.

Bob couldn't edit picture sets to save his life, and yet such was my liking for his work that I'd gladly undertake the task myself while paying for the beer. His affliction stemmed neither from any lack of understanding of his work or what magazine editors might want, but from fear of leaving out a crucial image. "Let's get rid of these," I'd politely suggest. To which the inevitable response would be, "but what if we need them?" To which I'd say: "Bob, the magazine is only 124 pages, and here are 4,000 transparencies." And so, I'd whittle down the mass of imagery to a generous handful of barnstormers with the promise that if I needed any more, I'd be in touch.

It sounds as though I have no sympathy for my friend. But I do, and in fact never more so than a few weeks ago when preparing a set for a pictorial in a travel magazine. Working on the basis that you should never file anything with a picture editor that you won't be happy to see in print, I hacked away diligently and methodically, and in my first pass reduced the portfolio to something more manageable. Encouraged, I flicked back and forth through the collection, weeding and pruning until I got it nicely down to a total of 36 (a number I hold in superstition, probably because it reminds me of my early days of shooting on 35 mm film, which confusingly yielded 36 frames per roll, or sometimes 37 if you were lucky.).

Three dozen photos might sound like a lot, but I was preparing imagery for several double-page spreads. As I checked over the keywords, captions and file names I started to imagine how the page layouts might eventually look. I was just about to hit the button to dispatch them into the ether when I realised an image had jumped ship, reducing me to an unlucky 35. This couldn't be tolerated and so, despite being on a tight deadline, I retraced my steps through the workflow history. Not being able to find the mutineer, I grabbed something innocuous from the master archive that looked passable, scrubbed it up a bit in my editing software, added it to the set, pressed the 'send' button and thought no more of it.

Why would I think any more of it? The magazine would never use such a photo in a million years. Or so I thought. That is, until I saw my article in print. And there it was, resplendent in all its glory as the opening shot of the lead feature. Which just goes to show that perhaps we aren't always the best judges of our own work, and that Bob might have had a point after all.

34

Why cameras really are as cheap as chips

There isn't a photographer alive who thinks cameras are reasonably priced. And yet, it's easy to make the case for our never having had it so good. Cameras may cost big bucks, but we're also in a Golden Age of value for money.

It is a truth universally acknowledged that nothing good ever came out of a conversation with an economist. And yet for all the universality of that acknowledgement, I recently found myself both in Toronto and spellbound as I listened to an economics professor telling me that photographers have never had it so good. Despite which, as I politely pretended to listen to him warbling on about 'money supply', I was secretly calculating when, if ever, I'd be in possession of sufficient cash surplus to buy myself a new camera. I know that professionals take a certain amount of pride in how battered their gear is, but my main instrument is now a Heath Robinson contraption held together by duct tape, safety pins and chewing gum. I'd dearly like to look like a proud and uncorrupted novice with a sleek, straight-from-the-box, new camera. But the truth is I can't afford one. Not today in any case.

My economist friend, who rejoices under the name of Zebedee, sensing my wandering attention, brought the conversation around to how he could help me go about getting a new camera. "You see," quoth he, "you might think that you can't afford one. But the truth is they've never been cheaper." He then bounced around lots of words such as cost, price, value and worth, which to my surprise, all mean different things and can have quite technical meanings. But what it all boiled down to was that while it might seem that we have to pay a lot of money for our cameras, pound for pound, in return we're getting something more substantial by several orders of magnitude than ever we'd have got a few decades ago. For the first time in my life I became interested in the subject of how money works.

You see, Zebedee explained, one of the governing principles of retail economics is that as soon as something becomes abundant then its price will fall. When energy became abundant – in the form of electricity – lighting our homes transformed overnight from being hugely expensive (using whale oil, paraffin, gas) to negligible. We never think about how much it costs to switch on an electric light because electricity is abundant and therefore cheap. Very good, I intoned, but where do cameras fit into all this?

Aha, returned the Canuck bean counter, explaining that something very similar happened in the photographic world. "All of a sudden, arithmetic went from being difficult to easy, specialist to generalist, scarce to abundant. With the arrival of the integrated circuit, binary maths became cheap. And because maths is the bedrock of electronic technology, taking photographs went from a process that was solved chemically, to one solved with strings of ones and zeros. Meanwhile, cameras equivalent to those that once cost several months' salary are now given away on your smartphone."

Not wishing to be thought a complete idiot I chipped in with my supposition that Moore's Law was probably at the root of this newfound abundance. To which he agreed whole-heartedly. "It's all about Moore's Law," he confirmed, before offering me the cautionary advice that there are now signs that the trend identified by Intel's legendary Gordon Moore in 1965 will slow down and come to an end. But not yet. For the moment at least, the idea still holds good that technology evolves at such a rate that you can double the number of transistors per square inch on an integrated circuit every two years. In layman's terms, any device that relies on a computer chip will double in its capacity or potency every two years, which is why we can now shoot 50-megapixel images at a rate of approaching ten frames per second on standard proprietary hardware. Twenty years ago, not even the most optimistic of futurologists were daring to dream of something that outrageous.

Which is all very nice, but I still can't afford my new camera. To which, Zebedee explained that I couldn't afford *not* to buy one post haste. Look at that heap of junk you call a camera, he gasped, estimating correctly that it was in the region of five years old. "It's nearly three generations of Moore's Law in the past. It's a museum piece. Today's cameras are shooting files more than twice the size yours can produce... and in the dark!"

In that, he was entirely correct. But I still wanted to know why, if Moore's Law is such a Good Thing, cameras haven't become cheaper. "Depends what you mean by 'cheaper'," said my friend (who was beginning to really annoy me.) "In general, no-one's going to put the price of any product down. But what they *will* do is give you tons more processing power because silicon chips are, well, as cheap as chips Also, because markets are competitive, manufacturers will cram as much silicon into their product as possible, which is why you can now shoot cinema-quality movies on your DSLR. If memory serves, I don't think that was something you could do on your medium format film camera that, back in the day, cost nearly as much as a small house."

Convincing and compelling, I had to agree, but hardly helpful, as I remained resolutely without the wherewithal to take advantage of my newly acquired fiscal knowledge. "You see," I ventured, "the real stumbling block is that I fundamentally don't have enough moolah to buy a new camera."

"You should have told me that a lot earlier in the piece," responded the much-amused social scientist. "If there's no money supply, no amount of economic theory is going to help you."

35

Seeing the City of Light
for the first time

Does there come a time when photographers simply can't summon up the energy to approach familiar subjects with a fresh eye? A quick trip to Paris left me in wide-eyed awe of my teenage daughter's ability to see past the clichés ...

Maybe it was the exquisite glass of Pouilly-Fumé that had put me in such an expansive mood of lavish generosity, but I promised my daughter that should she get a distinction in her ballet examination I'd take her to Paris for lunch. As soon as the words left my mouth, I started to regret my benevolence and realised I'd better get googling Eurostar *tout de suite*, for I knew there wasn't a hope in Hades of the stripling failing to achieve anything other than flying colours. While I was at it, I booked tickets for the Eiffel Tower, the Musée du Louvre and a table at an expensive restaurant on the Champs-Élysées. As I watched the hard-earned waving au revoir to my bank account, I flicked through a monograph of the great Parisian photographer of yesteryear, Eugène Atget, and started to plan our photo safari. After all, there's always something to photograph in Paris.

You see, apart from being a dancer of promise, the female teenager is also an irritatingly good photographer. And while she is a so-called 'digital native', endlessly shooting and editing on her Apple smartphone (she abandoned conventional cameras, if ever there were such things, a few years ago), she also has a taste for the retro, and is the proud owner of one of those johnny-come-lately restyled 'instant' cameras that regurgitate a rectangle of film that develops before your eyes. I had one of these things as a kid and, even then, I was convinced that it was terrible in every way. With a perspicacity beyond my years, I clearly remember all those years ago wondering if one day there would ever be an evolution in technology that would take film completely out of the equation. Okay, that's not actually true, and yet here we are today, instead of chucking all that superannuated nonsense in the bin, reviving old technology such as fountain pens, Space Invaders and 33rpm vinyl records.

Hot foot to the City of Light, because as Balzac said, if you don't visit Paris you can never be truly elegant. And elegant we were, father and daughter wandering around the artists' enclave of Montmartre, where I'd hung out drinking red wine and smoking *Gitanes* as a corduroy-jacketed student decades before. It was here that I hoped to snap a grainy street shot or two. Maybe a lingering glance of the Eiffel Tower at sunset. Or even some intriguing still lifes of shabby Citroën deux chevaux.

Armed with nothing more than my workhorse DSLR, onto which I'd bolted my favourite fast-and-wide lens, I sauntered, debonair and assured, certain that locked away somewhere in all the bits and bytes of my camera there was captive something quintessential: something that said as much about this great city as the novels of Émile Zola, Louis Aragon and Victor Hugo. As my daughter would say, "Good luck with that." Or whatever.

After every fishing trip there is the weigh-in, and once the sun had set, we decided to review our catch. On the one hand, here was I with a sorry portfolio of average junk that I knew would never make it past the digital waste-paper basket. On the other, there was the offspring with no less than a dazzling photoset on digital and film, both as fresh as a daisy. Well, to be honest, daisies didn't really get a look in. As I peered in frank admiration at the daring unconventionality of a rosy-cheeked ingénue, I realised that if this had been a fishing match, she would have beaten me hands down. For her keep-net was bulging with rare specimens, while mine could boast of nothing but half-starved minnows.

It's often said, though I have no idea by whom, that the worst moment of a man's life is when his son beats him at chess for the first time. And although my circumstances might on the face of it seem to be similar, they weren't. Rather than feeling that my parental authority had been usurped, I was overwhelmed by a sense of curiosity. How could these pictures be so good, when mine were derivative and clichéd? What had she done? And so, instead of sinking into a fit of morbid jealousy, I considered a line by William Wordsworth that reads, "the child is the father of the man," which to be correctly gender-aligned needs to be paraphrased. But you get the picture. Put more simply, as our transatlantic brethren would say, I'd been taken to school.

Now I've had a chance to mull this over, this is what I reckon might have happened. I think that the main difference between us wasn't a generation thing or a technology issue, or even an eye for detail or knack for composition. I'm sure that it all boils down to the fact that she had been excited to explore for the first time somewhere that to her was exotic, cool and wild. For me, despite my affection for Paris and fond memories of all the carefree experiences I have had there, it's just another city, another long haul on a train, another moment of pressure to produce acceptable photography that one day might pay for the Christmas turkey. But she had seized the day and, without the weight of the yoke of life's experience around her neck, seized it with both hands.

When the following day dawned, I decided that I'd take a leaf out of my daughter's photographic book and resolved to loosen up a little, to try a few things I'm normally too 'professional' to get involved with. And yet, while my photos improved marginally, the fact remains that this was one of those important occasions when innocence trumps experience.

36

Close encounters
of the leopard kind

*An assignment in the Kruger National Park yielded a
perfect series of encounters with that most elusive of big
cats, the leopard. After many years of unsuccessfully
trying to photograph them, I'd finally struck gold.*

It doesn't matter how much you pretend that birdlife,
flora and butterflies mean so much more to you, any visit
to South Africa's Kruger National Park is going to ignite
in all of us the desire to photograph the Big Five: leopard,
lion, Cape buffalo, African elephant and rhinoceros. They
are collectively so named because this is what the
moustachioed trophy-bagging, shotgun-toting 'great white
hunters' of yesteryear called them.

This label has nothing to do specifically with size, but
more the difficulty and danger that went with tracking
them down for the kill. We still call them the Big Five, as
a reminder that these days we shoot animals with

cameras, not guns. We care about their conservation and the preservation of their habitat. And we like to spend time with them.

I can't put my finger on why, but my favourite of them all is the leopard. Ever since I read Jim Corbett's stupendous *The Man-Eating Leopard of Rudraprayag* as a kid, I've been both a fan of Corbett and these slinky felines. And while his book is about one man's quest to kill the aforementioned cat, Corbett's account, instead of leaving me filled with horror at the thought of putting a bullet between its eyes, left me with nothing but increased admiration for the spotted quadruped, and I've collected books on leopards all my adult life. (I even edited an anthology of leopard literature, and complained bitterly when I was overruled on the issue of whether to include Vita Sackville-West's wonderful poem *Leopards at Knole* that describes "leopards on the gable-ends, leopards on the painted stair" at her stately pile in Kent.)

I think possibly one of the reasons I was able to forgive Corbett for blowing out the brains of the man-eater of Rudraprayag was that, in one of those poacher-turned-gamekeeper moments, the archetypal great white hunter and friend of the Queen, was to in later life have a road to Damascus revelation in which he put the double-barrelled rifle out to grass in order to become a conservationist. In the process he made history as one of the first photographers to use the camera as a tool for raising awareness for wildlife welfare. Quite rightly, the pith-helmeted corporal of the British Indian Army gives his name to the sub-continent's first national park. And also quite rightly, is he regarded as one of the forefathers of both wildlife protection and wildlife photography.

I can only assume that he had better luck photographing leopards than I did, and that is because, during the quarter of a century I've been roaming the African bush, I've not taken one leopard shot of note. For sure, in Kenya I've seen them asleep in trees half a mile away, obscured in the shadows. In Namibia I've seen rehab leopards that are virtually as tame as your domestic moggy (one in particular – the instantly recognisable 'Wahu' at the AfriCat Foundation in Okonjima – routinely features, unfairly I'd have thought, in wildlife photography competitions). And once in Botswana I even saw the disturbing sight of a leopard that had been badly mangled in a fight, scavenging in the open for food in broad daylight. But never had I seen a truly wild, fit and active leopard on the move, and I'd never seen one on the hunt. And so, when the call came before dawn during a recent trip to Kruger, informing me that there was a two-year-old female leopard in the area and we should go to see what she was up to, my senses stirred, while secretly holding no great hope of a meaningful encounter.

But meaningful encounter we had, for there, just after sunrise, sitting atop a termite mound sniffing the air, was the leopard to define a leopard's grace. Although it was quite unusual to see one hunting at dawn, it's not unheard of, and so to watch this sleek feline stretch into action, tracking a small group of impala under cover of a ravine, was a life-changing experience.

Exhilarated, I bagged a few terrific portraits and some stalking shots of the mottled, tawny cat among the sand-coloured winter savannah, my hands slightly trembling with the thrill of it all. The hunt failed, as morning hunts so often do, mainly because the leopard mistimed its move, causing the impala to flee like lightning in all directions. It all happened so quickly everything was out of focus. But I was fortunate in that, over the next few days, my leopard encounters were so frequent that at one point I decided to lighten the workload a little by photographing red-billed hornbills, Burchell's starlings and lilac-breasted rollers.

On returning home, I quickly edited a few of the more significant barnstormers and proudly showed them to my daughter, who is a keen animal rights supporter and strident vegetarian. "Wow, Dad," intoned the juvenile female human: "cool cheetahs." Okay, so that's a mistake anyone can make. But, considering that her favourite book was once Rudyard Kipling's *Just So Stories*, and doubly considering our favourite story was 'How the Leopard Got His Spots', I thought this a little slack.

On the other hand, it presented the perfect opportunity for us to sit together and read once again that sumptuous collection of folk tales that has in its first sentence those immortal words:

"... once upon a time, O my Best Beloved."

37

Long hot summer ends in laptop meltdown

While most photographers tend to enjoy endless feasts of sunshine, the record-breaking long hot summer of 2018 was a bridge too far for my trusty old laptop that fried in the heat, nearly at the cost of an important photoset...

You wouldn't normally expect the first telephone call on a Monday morning to be a pleasant one, and so on picking up the receiver I was relieved to hear the soothing tones of a magazine editor friend who was casting the speculative net, hoping to catch a picture feature about somewhere hot. "Bit of a flap here. Have you got anything we can turn around quickly?" she asked. Affirmative, came my reply: "Is Libya hot enough?" I then explained that while meteorologists bicker endlessly over whether Death Valley is hotter, the small Libyan town of 'Aziziya was recognised for almost a century as the hottest place on earth. Having notched up an eye-watering 58C (that's

136.4F in old money), 'Aziziya has now been demoted as a result of some retrofitted scientific mumbo-jumbo as obscure as the LBW law.

I've been lucky enough to travel in Libya on several occasions and am further blessed in that I have a laptop stuffed with images of camel fairs, Roman ruins and coppersmiths in the Medina. My editor friend thought this perfect, adding that the quicker I filed the story, the happier she'd be and the richer I'd become. Then the line went dead as if she'd mysteriously predicted that I was about to engage her further, explaining the controversy that developed in 2012, when a specialist from the World Meteorological Organization claimed that the climatologist that took the original reading 90 years previously (to the day) had been unqualified to read a thermometer. With 'Aziziya thus scratched from the list of runners and riders, the laurels were handed back to Death Valley on a technicality.

Sensing time's wingèd chariot hurrying near, I decided to disregard all distractions and go about editing my photoset without further ado. I opened up the post-processing software in a flurry of efficiency, and within an hour was knee-deep in editing. Before the hour was up something had gone quietly wrong and my computer was dead. It would help me to attain peace of mind if I could say it exploded and there were jets of flame and plumes of smoke everywhere, priests with holy books and a cortège of mourners. But there was nothing. Just a dull black screen and a rats' nest of switched-over cables, as I hoped against hope that the problem was anywhere other than inside my computer. Where once there was a digital image of Leptis Magna, now there were ruins.

It was the work of a few phone calls to establish that the flimsy hope I'd entertained had been in vain, and so I trudged, like a reluctant schoolboy returning to class after the summer hols, down the hill to the local computer specialist. The guru in question was a smashing chap called Ajay, who told me not to worry about a thing. Somewhat worryingly, Ajay sniffed the USB ports and asked me lots of invasive questions, leaving me feeling as though I was being interrogated by one of those boring doctors that insist on asking tiresome questions about how many units of alcohol you ingest in a week.

"Don't worry," Ajay reassured me, "everyone lies. We'll get you up and running in no time." What he meant by this was that I urgently needed a replacement system management controller (I didn't even know I had one), an ultrasonic clean of the logic board (unfair, as I hadn't even spilt wine on this one) and a few other tweaks and twiddles that brought, in line with Ajay's predictions, the machine back up to showroom spec.

With a butcher's bill of four hundred pounds, I decided that Ajay owed me some sort of explanation for what had caused the failure of the computer beyond his general demeanour that implied to my paranoid state of mind that he thought photographers were idiots. "Your machine was corroding internally due to moisture, which caused a short circuit, and after that everything went kaput." I retaliated that to the best of my knowledge, after the Chilean red wine incident of 2014 on a previous laptop, this unit had been steadfastly teetotal. He looked at me once more like a doctor doubting his patient, before saying: "This was condensation. Been anywhere humid recently?"

As a matter of fact, I'd just returned from a photographic trip to Mediterranean Spain, I explained, where it was 40C at midnight, not a breath of wind and with a level of humidity that meant you could never get your hands dry. "That will have done it," he said, barely containing the note of self-congratulation in his voice.

I must have looked pretty baleful, doleful and wan at the same time. In what I think might have been an attempt to raise my deflated spirits, he uttered the words: "Could have been worse. Could have been the hard drive."

As I trudged back up the hill, I felt a degree of misplaced misanthropy towards the technician that had saved my laptop and had got me back to editing my photos without so much as the loss of a pixel. Within twenty-four hours of my Libya photoset disappearing before my eyes, here it was again shining on the screen. There was the camel fair at Ghadames. There was the Red Castle at Tripoli. There were the Berber grain stores in the desert. All waiting to be tidied up and dispatched to the magazine that would eventually print them, get them into the economy and convert them into maybe, if I was lucky, sufficient coin of the realm to pay for the repair to my laptop.

38
Hoodwinked on the streets of Vilnius

An assignment to the Lithuanian capital of Vilnius reveals that there are times when we need to treat our subjects with a certain amount of caution. As I found out, you can be too trusting, and things might not be what they seem...

The part of me that enjoys the cultural tropes of Soviet Constructivism and agitprop underground movements railing against oligarchical collectivism, naively hoped that Lithuania's capital city Vilnius would be just like that stylised idiom so brilliantly rendered by George Orwell in *Nineteen Eighty-Four*.

But alas, the city was a modern cosmopolitan affair, with wide elegant boulevards, boutiques selling amber, and trendy roadside cafes in such abundance that there seemed to be a pressing need to coin a collective noun for them. Even the restored historical sites of the Second World War – the ghettos, churches and public squares –

had an air of recently having been royally primped for a photographic spread in a glossy travel magazine.

I only had one camera with me, and only one lens. There'd been one of those tedious kerfuffles at Heathrow in which an unfortunate traveller had left an item of luggage unattended for a fraction of a second, the result of which was that the entire British aviation infrastructure had ground to a halt. As with all situations like this, the victims are blamed and punished, meaning that I received a communication from the airline telling me that passengers were to bring nothing with them other than hand luggage. Nothing could be checked in, and in fact, it would save everyone a lot of inconvenience if you decided not to travel at all. After several hours of witnessing the emotional temperature of an entire airport rise by the second, I boarded my plane. By the time I was looking down on the extraordinary Curonian Spit that threads like a necklace across the Baltic Sea from Russia to Lithuania, I could feel my creative temperament returning to something like equilibrium, with Heathrow, as ever, a barely-suppressed memory that will for ever return to haunt my sleepless nights.

With but one camera and lens I felt like one of those street photographers you read about. Soon enough I was walking along the cobbled streets of Vilnius that are positively festooned with accordion players wearing berets, bad portrait artists also in berets and vendors of candy floss, many of which sported berets too. Despite the proliferation of berets, I took to the procedure like a duck to water, and my camera started to fill with the carefully crafted clichés that had been laid out before me by the local tourism authorities who, presumably thinking that photographers these days can't bear too much reality, had decided to present their historical city as though it had been dreamed up by Walt Disney.

But it wasn't all glitz and chintz, for lurking at the shadowy fringes of an outdoor market sat a lonely, dishevelled, hunched figure wearing a battered old greatcoat and what I took to be a Russian Army cap. And while I've no experience in the discipline of phaleristics, even I could see that this noble war veteran was selling his campaign medals on the street. There was a story in this, I thought, and so I approached him. I won't presume to bore you with how we managed to achieve the following conversation in Russian, English and sign language. But basically the nuts and bolts are that I asked him if I could take a photograph of him and he said that I could, providing I bought one of his medals.

This is the point at which students of moral philosophy will start drawing lines in the sand and chuntering on about the ethics of the situation. But, as I wanted the shot and he wanted the money, I dispensed the requisite sum in euros (he flatly refused local litai), trousered the medal and got snapping, all the while feeling a bit queasy, pretty certain that I was exploiting the misery of a fellow human. After a while he became bored, made a very easily understood gesture and the shoot was over. As I walked a few paces away from the man, I realised that I had to do the decent thing and return his medal to him. Even though I like to think of myself as financially underwhelmed at all times, here in the West we have so much, while this ancient soldier had so little. This man had served his country, was living on the streets and was selling his most valuable possessions to buy bread.

To this day I still want to believe that. But I can't, because right on cue a policeman strode up, addressing me in perfect English while barking something unpleasant in Russian to the man who by now needs inverted commas around the term 'war veteran'. He's a conman, quoth the gendarme, explaining to me that the person over whom I'd suffered so much 'photographer's guilt', was a well-known cutpurse, rapscallion and ne'er-do-well that made a living by emotionally extorting donations from sympathetic tourists and photographers. Furthermore, he had a Tupperware box full of medals he'd stolen from a respectable numismatist on the other side of town, only no one could wrangle up sufficient evidence to justify pressing charges. By night, I thought, he probably trod the boards as Hamlet at the nearby Lithuanian National Drama Theatre.

To say I felt sheepish is unfair on sheep, which I suspect of being less gullible than I. After swopping back the medal for the money under the watchful eye of the constabulary, I wandered off annoyed, and not just because I'd been hoodwinked. It was because yet another seed of doubt had been sown in my mind, another veil of cynicism had been drawn over my eyes. It can be a hard enough job at times, without having to question the authenticity of everything before you.

39

Hooked on the art of fishing photography

On the surface, photography and fishing share several characteristics, such as dedication, patience, technique. The deeper you go into it, the more they have in common, as I discovered on a recent angling trip to West Wales...

There can be few better metaphors for photography than that of the art of coarse fishing. Angling with rod and line in an attempt to outwit freshwater fish requires patience, technique, dedication and, as I was to become only too aware, both physical fitness and a whole arsenal of expensive equipment. I made these discoveries recently as the result of a conversation I had with an old friend in the local watering hole. I knew that Neil was a fiendishly good match fisherman specialising in carp, because many is the time I've admired his snaps of prime specimens of the *Cyprinidae* family on his smartphone. If I read the *Angler's Mail* today as assiduously as I once did as a fishing-obsessed teenager, I'd have also been able to admire Neil's lofty rankings in regional competition result tables.

And so, it wasn't with the usual feeling of doom that I heard a discourse starting with the words "you're a photographer, aren't you?" floating across the evening air at my local. Realising it was Neil inviting me to join him on a day trip to Pembrokeshire with my camera, the ears twitched and I replied with an enthusiastic positive. I've always loved fishing and I don't do it enough.

"There is one condition," I ventured. Before committing to departing at some godforsaken hour, I would need his assurance that I'd get the chance of a cast or two and catch a carp for myself. To which he agreed. When asked to be more specific about our destination, he told me we were headed for Holgan Farm in Llawhaden, nearest town… well, there wasn't one really. What might be of more interest was that the fishery was owned by former World Champion Ian Heaps, and we'd be sure to find a few moments to chat with him over a cup of tea.

Sensing a payday of sorts in the offing, I telephoned the editor of a Welsh lifestyle magazine and before long I was in business. I'd write a 'Local Hero' profile on Heaps, along with a review of the fishery as seen through the eyes of specimen-hunter Neil, both of whom were to be photographed by myself.

As the appointed day dawned fair and blithe, my spirits soared and we sallied westward in Neil's transit van, swopping good-natured middle-aged banter about how both photography and fishing have changed for the worse since we first started. Furthermore, I joked that his craft amounted to no more than drowning worms while dozing with a can of beer in your hand, and he retaliated by claiming mine was the triumph of staying awake while occasionally pressing a switch. High spirits indeed.

I remember Ian Heaps from the front page of the *Angler's Mail* in the mid-1970s when he won the world title on a canal in Poland. Heaps was happy to relive the day for me in words. But he also showed me with much pride a fantastic photograph in which there was literally row upon row of spectators on the opposite bank from where he was fishing.

"There were 30,000 at that match," recalled Heaps, "shouting *'Olé'* every time I landed a fish, and sighing whenever I missed a bite." To cut a long story short, Heaps made a pile of cash out of fishing, which he was to invest in his childhood dream of designing his own fishery in every detail. The project took him a quarter of a century to complete. The result is one of the finest and most picturesque suites of fishing lakes in the UK.

As Neil and I set up our gear on adjacent pegs, the thought occurred to me that the process of preparing for our day ahead was remarkably similar, the one exception being that by the time he was ready for action there wasn't a great deal of difference between where Neil was sitting and Mission Control at the Space Center Houston. With the sun in the east, while Neil waited for the float to dip below the surface, I waited for the clouds to clear. While he continually moved the game along by switching baits, swims, techniques and rods, I toggled between cameras, lenses, angles and settings. We were doing exactly the same thing: Neil was catching the fish, while I was catching Neil catching the fish. Later, as the temperature drained from the day, we agreed that we'd both got what we came for and it was time to go home to review the day's catch over a pint. "But before we go," said Neil "it's your turn."

If anybody ever tells you that carp fishing is easy and that, as is the common fallacy, docile specimens form an orderly queue to give themselves up, tell them that they don't know what they're talking about. After spending a blank hour of holding a 16m pole motionless, my back aching and my eyes swimming from the concentration, I was ready to call it quits. And yet, after several missed bites, I just about managed to hook one, and after a battle that took ten minutes and that still hurts my shoulder muscles, landed a 12lb specimen.

"I don't know how you can do that all day," I said in admiration. "I thought angling for carp was going to be relaxing, simple and fun." He replied that having seen what I'd been through that day just to get 'a few shots' for a local magazine, he could quite easily say the same thing about me.

40

Turning the tables on the outdoor photographer

*Oddly enough, outdoor photography isn't always about
taking photographs outdoors. Sometimes it involves
taking a portrait of an outdoor photographer – an
experience that can be both disconcerting and rewarding.*

Of all the recurrent nightmares to fret the silence of the
night, perhaps the most frightening – in photographic
terms at least – is that of being required to photograph a
photographer, especially, and let's not beat about the bush
here, one who is of exalted status.

I admit I don't have this particular nightmare very often,
but when the picture editor at the other end of the
telephone line informed me that my mission, should I
choose to accept it, was to take a portrait of a senior polar
photographer, one that "that really says something about
who he is, what he does and where he goes", the throat
tightened and the eyes swivelled in their sockets. At the

same time a discomfiture developed in the lower regions of the digestive tract in a manner not dissimilar to that which occurs the night before your French A-Level examination for which you've done no revision.

If you have anything more than even the faintest of passing interest in the world of expedition photography you'll know Gerard's work, and probably know it well. For his are the images that find their way to the front covers of travel magazines and coffee table books, those vast displays in Waterloo Station or the grounds of the Natural History Museum, town squares in Scandinavia and the big screens of fabled lecture halls. Such is the grandeur of his polar iconography that Gerry (according to strong and persistent rumour) had once been invited to chair the judging panel on an international photography competition simply to stop him winning it for a third year in succession. So, you get the picture. He's handsomely adept at what he does, and my job was to take a portrait of the man that, in the time-honoured tradition of proper portraiture, went beyond a likeness of someone's face.

The one thing I had in my favour was that I knew Gerry quite well and had even commissioned his photographic services a few times for various magazines I'd edited over the years. And so, after the opening telephonic greetings he was swiftly of a mind to invite me to his Bristol studio where we could get the job done. As it dawned on me that he was taking the exercise seriously and was far removed from finding it beneath his dignity to be snapped by a photographer I assumed he'd think a jobbing hack, my confidence rose. I explained that the portrait was to be outside in natural light, preferably with something nautical in the background. I further explained that we would need to include a prop that established the polar connection, but which didn't pull focus from the fact that the composition was a portrait. Oh, and we needed to do get it all done tomorrow, which was a hassle (for me at least) because the portrait lens to which I attach almost supernatural, nay talismanic, faith was in dock being serviced. "Don't worry about any of that," he said. "Use my camera. Travel light and we can go to the pub after."

I found it extraordinary that Gerry knew next-to-nothing about how to sit for a portrait. But on the other hand he, I suppose obviously, knew a lot about assisting on a shoot, and before long I was in the oddly seamless scenario where my subject was also my assistant. Which was handy because I was briskly to reach the understanding that, having used cameras by one specific Japanese manufacturer for more than a quarter of a century, trying to get to grips with the controls on an instrument manufactured by the *other* main Japanese camera-maker was nowhere near as instinctive as I thought it might be. We set up the shot – the prop, incidentally, was a hard-shell waterproof camera case festooned with expedition sponsor stickers – and after depressing the shutter-release button merely 14 times in three minutes, the shoot was over. "That's it," I informed Gerry. "That's it?" he replied in surprise. "Yup, I've got the shot."

Later, as we sat on the banks of the Avon watching the sun dip below the horizon, polishing off a few glasses of the cold and frothy, Gerry turned to me and asked why I'd taken so few exposures. The long and the short of it, I explained, feeling like a student sharing his naïve insights with a world-weary tutor who had seen it all before, is that I've spent my entire digital career filling data cards with files I know I'll never use. Experience has taught me that when it comes to portraits, providing you've got everything in place and everyone's relaxed, you'll get your best shots in the first few minutes. After that, I continue as a cosmetic exercise to create the illusion that the whole event is important and that I'm a professional.

"But since you're a photographer and know what's going on, I didn't really feel the need to sustain the illusion. Just imagine the state of affairs," I persisted, "if Jackson Pollock had carried on after he knew he'd finished."

Gerry conceded that there was indeed a lot to be said for my argument because, "the most important thing about all this is to trust your judgement." As we walked to the railway station, he suddenly stopped and got his camera out of its case, from which Gerry extracted the data card. He handed it to me with a laugh, saying: "Here, take this. Something tells me you're going to need it."

41

Prickly problems
with silhouettes

You won't get very far in taking a decent silhouette if you don't plan your shot to the last detail. From Easter Island to Arizona, snagging silhouettes is fraught with mishap, as I discovered on two memorable occasions...

When it comes to the silhouette, the world is evenly divided between those who consider it a credible weapon in the photographic armoury, and those who don't. For some reason I can't quite put my finger on, the silhouette is a subject that elicits extremes of emotion, without very much middle ground. I've never met a photographer who says they're *okay-ish*.

I make no apology for being of the former camp. As much as I am drawn to light, I am drawn to shadows, and to see what is essentially a shadow in the sky is for me a 'moth-to-a-flame' moment. When people tell me they don't like silhouettes I routinely ask their opinion of total eclipses, which we may poetically describe as a silhouette of the moon. Because everyone likes an eclipse, I nearly always win the exchange. But I take no joy in victory, for people with no love of, say, silhouettes of Easter Island's *Moai* statuary, are sadly missing out.

And so, when the commission came to shoot a portfolio of Easter Island for a travel magazine, I could barely believe my luck. I know you're supposed to take these matters in your stride, maintaining an exterior of nonchalance, but the idea of flying into the heart of the South Pacific Ocean to realise a childhood dream of seeing what should be one of the Wonders of the World, was beyond belief. In a fit of excitement, I decided there and then to plan the entire expedition down to the finest jot and tittle. First up: learn how to take a decent silhouette. By luck, the magazine I was editing at the time had on its front cover that very month a silhouette of polar adventurer Ben Saunders scrambling over a pressure ridge, shot by the ice master himself, Martin Hartley. I phoned Hartley and told him I needed a crash course in silhouettery. Hours later, after settling an enormous tab at Soho's *Dog & Duck*, I walked away with the bluff Lancastrian's taciturn advice to: "Get the sun behind your subject and 'stop down', " by which he meant I should twiddle one of those fiendishly complicated dials on top of the camera to allow less light into the instrument.

The long haul to Easter Island via Madrid and Santiago became a short haul when I fell at the first fence. An air-traffic control snafu at Adolfo Suárez Madrid–Barajas Airport meant that I missed my connection to Chile and thus, having come to the realisation that my expedition to Easter Island was over before it had barely begun, I trudged back to Heathrow, spitting blood. If there was anything positive circulating in my mind at all, it certainly wasn't the prospect of shooting silhouettes of *Moai*. In fact, I forgot all about silhouettes. That is until late 2018, when I found myself deep in Arizona's Sonoran Desert.

Of the many things this wonderful wasteland has going for it, perhaps the most visually attractive to the photographer is the saguaro cactus which enjoys totemic status in that part of the world, not just because of its imposing size and surreal appearance, but because the *Carnegiea gigantean* is native to the region. While we might be accustomed to seeing its classic profile as a cultural trope of gun-slinging movies of the Wild West in general, the chances are we're watching a botanical and geographical anomaly. This is because the saguaro only grows in the Sonoran Desert, which is only in Arizona and Mexico. When we see such cactuses adorning the labels of Tex-Mex hot sauce bottles, what we have is a mild case of ethnic appropriation. But it seems the good people of Arizona have far more important matters on their minds.

Arizona is an 'open carry' state, which means that you are legally entitled to carry a gun providing it is visible on your person, 'carried' in a holster or similar. You can't carry one in your hand because this is technically 'brandishing', an activity frowned upon to the extent that the gendarmerie regards this as an outright crime. The State of Arizona also frowns on people shooting their beloved cactuses to the point where a persistent (and false) rumour exists that anyone discharging their firearm at a saguaro could find themselves in the clink for a quarter of a century (the class four felony of 'cactus plugging', in fact, carries a maximum sentence of three years and nine months). It follows that if you are going to shoot a saguaro, it's best you do so with a camera.

It took me two days to get a decent silhouette of my saguaro. Despite the Sonoran Desert being generously populated with these gargantuan spiny succulents, it took some serious scouting to find a specimen of sufficient grandeur for my purposes in a suitable location, the specifics of which were quite, well, specific. As I intended to shoot at sunrise, I needed a clear line-of-sight of the eastern horizon, preferably from an elevated viewpoint, with the terrain to the east of my cactus declining in altitude towards a mountain ridge containing, if not drama, then at least a few pronounced serrations.

But that's what location scouting is all about, and despite the fact that I'd set myself a pretty tall order, I succeeded in finding what I was looking for at the Tom's Thumb trailhead in the McDowell Sonoran Conservancy. With Hartley's words still resonating in my mind, and after a few false starts that included several irritating delays while I waited for aeroplane contrails to clear, I got my shot. And, though I say so myself, the final image was a triumph. But I suspect only half of you would agree.

42

More mysteries of the missing cameras

*We mislay trivial belongings with such startling
regularity it's tempting to think that there might be
something wrong with the evolution of the human mind.
But that could never apply to cameras, could it?*

It was towards the end of the last millennium, when I
was the editor of *BBC Focus* magazine, that my trusty and
faithful deputy strode into my rabbit-hutch office and
dropped the bombshell. It wasn't so much that he wished
to enter into a matrimonial contract with his bride-to-be
that created the shockwave. I thoroughly approved of the
union and said as much with the words, if I remember
correctly, "quite right, too." It was more the idea that he
wished to remove himself from the editorial office for a
fortnight in order to visit Mexico on honeymoon. The
blood drained from my body as I realised I was staring
down the barrel at two weeks of editorial grunt-work, as

opposed to my more usual management style, the principal component of which was to walk around the office waving my arms about while informing everyone that they were all doing very well.

And so, you can imagine I welcomed Denzel's long-awaited return to the scriptorium with the sort of fanfare generally reserved for the Prodigal Son. After the fatted calf had been slaughtered (okay, a few pints of the good stuff had been sunk in Soho's *Dog & Duck*), I asked him with as much epithalamic gusto as could be mustered how the honeymoon had gone. The upshot was that all had gone to plan, apart from the slight worm-in-the-apple of the newly-minted couple having their camera pinched at the ancient Mesoamerican city of Teotihuacan. "How on earth did that happen?" I enquired, for to be honest, as much as I enjoy the occasional tale of wedded bliss, I much prefer photographic intrigue.

There then followed a tale that, had it not been from the horse's mouth (thus placing it squarely in what historians call the 'criterion of embarrassment'), could hardly have been believed. It turns out that Denzel had asked some local teenagers to take a photograph of the recently spliced dyad in front of some romantic ruins, whereupon the teenagers in question simply legged it – with said camera – never to be seen again. I thought long and hard, looked at my doleful deputy, and with as much compassion as I could dredge up from the depths of my soul said: "Well, don't think for a minute you can put that on your expenses."

Looking back at this unhappy tale, I'm sorry to report that this is but one of several incidents in my close experience when cameras have gone walkabout due to the gullibility, naivety and stupidity of their owners. I will immediately put my hand up and admit that once, while on assignment in New York, I was so inattentive to the context I found myself in that I jumped out of a Yellow Cab, only to watch it disappear down 42nd Street with my entire kit still on the back seat, and as with the previous anecdote, 'never to be seen again.' The tedious result of which was, the following morning, a visit to the glorious B&H photographic retailer just off 8th Avenue, which under normal circumstances constitutes nothing short of a photographer's house of worship.

If we call that simple negligence, then there is the related syndrome of too much trust in your surroundings. Pity poor Ted, who only left his backpack on the floor in his local for a moment while ordering a pint. When he looked down the bag had gone. He knew everyone in the by now unsuitably named *Live and Let Live*, but soon learned the hard way that when it comes to human greed you can't really trust anyone. The constabulary couldn't have cared less, and when Ted saw his camera in a high street pawnshop window, neither did the proprietor of the establishment under review. Chastened and humiliated, Ted is now a shadow of his former self and resembles one of those wraiths in *The Lord of the Rings*.

While there's no need to tell the story again of how I packed a spare camera body into my check-in luggage on the overnight flight to Johannesburg, and while there is no need to repeat the sequence of the events that led my friend Bunsen to become separated from his camera in the city of Harbin in northern China, it might be worth bringing up the ballad of how I lost (yet another) gadget bag at the Ezeiza International Airport in Buenos Aires.

This was a classic, and as the underlying cause was exhaustion and there was no alcohol involved whatsoever, I can with a certain amount of self-defence claim that after having *two* bags x-rayed in the security zone, I *forgot* to pick up one of them. This I didn't realise until after I'd cleared the immigration desk, by which point it was too late to turn back. I was no longer in Argentina and nothing could be done. A few months later I was astonished to discover that my bag, along with all of its contents, had made its circuitous way to the Royal Geographical Society in London where we were reunited.

Then there was the time when polar photographer Martin Hartley and I managed to lose one of his cameras at a wedding in the south of France... But that story is such a gem I'm going to keep it for another time. For the moment, let's just leave it at this: while Denzel may have been guilty of startling gullibility on his honeymoon, he was by no means the first and, I can absolutely guarantee, he won't be the last.

43

Exploited by the appeal to photographic charity

From time to time we all feel the call to donate an image or two to a charity in support of a worthy cause. There are also times, as I discovered, when our attempts to do the decent thing come undone and end in an ethical mess.

It would be a churl that didn't dip the hand into the pocket every now and then to dispense a little something to charity in return for a warm fuzzy feeling. I know that I certainly have no objection to the occasional bit of *pro bono* work, especially if I can achieve such philanthropy by, to use the horrible modern phrase, 'repurposing assets'. It takes little of my time and to specialist charities, such Samaritan acts can make a world of difference.

In common with virtually every photographer of my acquaintance, I don't have much cash to sprinkle around. But I do have a ton of useful photographic stock, and you're welcome. But there are grey areas to consider, even when making the world a better place. For instance, I recently received an email from the chief executive of a large commercial organisation asking me as a favour to donate a portrait I'd shot of him. This would be printed in a mind-bogglingly dull 'environmental impact assessment report' commissioned by his organisation, along with the social media marketing that supported it. As my personal ethics tend to lead me to being helpful, I sent the digital file to the grey-suited businessman without the loss of a moment. Even if the whole procedure did feel somewhat tangential to a bona fide charitable cause, my image would be used positively in the context of sustainable development and my duty to the planet would have been discharged. Though I have now seen that image all over the internet in connection with said organisation, I never received a single word of thanks.

Fast forward to a few weeks later when I was at an industry luncheon. There present was the same grey-suited executive in question, whose demeanour led me to suppose he was avoiding eye contact with me. So I went up to him and, as politely as I could, re-introduced myself before expressing mild surprise that while he'd enjoyed the benefits of my photograph, I'd somehow missed his bouquet thanking me for doing the decent thing and assisting him in keeping down the production costs of his report. His response was as follows: "I don't owe you any thanks. You'd already taken the picture and you've been paid for it. So far as I can see, it was just lying around doing nothing…" He continued by questioning my mental stability, accused me of being a snowflake and suggested I join a netball team. Unbelievable really.

Now, the author of the book you are holding in your hands is possessed of too much in the way of Old School manners to even countenance reproducing my eventual reply in print. So, we'll leave it at having been initially lost for words, when I eventually found them, I retorted with a strafing of fruity intensifiers derived from what people assume to be Anglo-Saxon, but is strictly speaking Old English. After what seemed like a quarter of an hour, and satisfied that I had exhausted my vituperative arsenal, I span on my heel and with a final 'damn your duckpond' withdrew from his company with, I have to say, very little in the way of regret.

Although I expected to, I didn't feel better at all. Much worse, in fact. Not because I'd spoken in frank terms to a man who unquestionably deserved it, but because I'd sunk to the level of what I assume he might feel are his 'standards', while temporarily abandoning mine. You'll think this is all a bit holier-than-thou, but my experience of photographers is that the overwhelming majority of us is made up of a smashing bunch of men and women who simply don't go around behaving like these aggressive, ethically-challenged, alpha-type thugs. I let the side down there, gentle reader, and I apologise for misrepresenting our peaceful tribe.

Now that the storm clouds have abated and made way for my more habitual sunny disposition, I can say that I've gained some perspective on the matter. That's because I've never had any problem with giving away the occasional image to charity, and I'm sure most of you support good causes in a similar way. It makes me feel a little less guilty about my taken-for-granted Western affluence, personal security, right to vote, public transport (*that's plenty – ed*) to know that there is one less kid in Zanzibar with blackwater fever, an acre or two more of the rainforest under protection, or a penguin's medical bills taken care of as a result of my largesse. It costs me nothing and the whole exercise gets filed in the 'least I could do' section of my brain. I admire people who work for charities and I want to help them.

But I don't admire those crashingly boring executives whose only management technique is to be as hostile as possible in pursuit of profit. So, by the time the individual under review had completed his trifecta of blatant rudeness, bloody-minded autocracy and obvious theft, I discovered not unreasonably, I think, that my nose was a sixteenth of an inch out of joint. He didn't give a damn about the way he'd treated me, and here was I seriously considering apologising to him (for the record, I stuck to my guns and didn't.)

So that's it. I've learned my lesson. No more charity from me. That's not true, of course, for I think we are all under a duty to believe St Francis of Assisi when he said: "where there is charity and wisdom there is neither fear nor ignorance." It's a sentiment I cordially invite my businessman friend to consider at length. I'll even extend my sense of charity to lending him my dictionary for when he gets confused by any of the big words.

44

Mental pictures of the 'Heart of Wales'

With one of the most celebrated of railway lines starting on my doorstep, I was determined to take advantage of the opportunity and produce a portfolio of the seldom-seen corners of Wales. But it didn't go quite as expected.

We're told by experts on the subject that one of the finest scenic railways in these sceptred isles is the 'Heart of Wales' line from Glamorgan to Shropshire. As often as I have read this, or indeed marvelled at Michael Portillo's presentation of it on his *Great British Railway Journeys* TV programme, I have said to myself: "Do you know, one of these days I'm going to photograph that." But I never have, which is an embarrassment, because I come from Swansea, where the current version of the line starts, and have friends in Church Stretton, one stop from its end.

New Year's resolutions are fine things and since over the ages I've made a successful tradition of them, there was nothing for it. Without further ado, I packed the cameras and sandwiches in equal measure by weight, and duly trundled off to Swansea station, from where I'd catch the quaintly antiquated single-carriage locomotive in my quest for the real Wales.

There is a fantastic poem by Edward Thomas that describes an uneventful railway journey, during which his train makes an unscheduled stop in the sleepy village of Adlestrop. At first glance the poem is hardly about anything at all: just a nostalgic line or two about an old-fashioned Edwardian idea of England. But on repeated readings – I first fell under its spell decades ago – it reveals itself as a moment when the clocks stopped, allowing the poet to be distracted by the songs of 'all the birds of Oxfordshire and Gloucestershire.' This delicate recollection has found its way into the literary canon not just for its colloquial lyricism, but also because, written immediately before the outbreak of the Great War, it seems to capture Elgar or Finzi's England, the defence of which would cost so many lives, including that of the poet himself. It's now wrongly considered a 'war poem'.

If you think that in our brutally digitalised world there are no such moments left to be had, then perhaps it is time to take the train. For, as my time-worn engine threaded its way north through the very bones of pre-industrialised Wales, virtually every station stop (a lot of which are charmingly 'request halts') provided an 'Adlestrop' all of its own, in which the birds of English counties became the herons, ospreys and kites of Carmarthenshire and Radnorshire.

I use the historic county names because the modern Dyfed and Powys don't quite express what was happening in my mind, or Thomas' poem either. The train really did go clickety-clack in the old-fashioned way, and so too did my imagination as I wondered how I could capture that feeling of sepia-infused time in two dimensions with anything like the same spirit as that marvellous poem.

I imagine most people simply don't realise how rural and wild Wales is, and that's because everyone drives everywhere in cars. But from the train, you soon realise that once you get north of the M4 corridor, that boundary between the Industrial Revolution and the agrarian Wales of centuries past, there is a feast of mountains and rivers, pasture and forest: all of it begging to be photographed. I nearly added 'before it is too late', but there seems to be something so well organised about the country's geological defences that the 'Land of My Fathers' can remain quietly and confidently safe from the world of semiconductors. With one exception, and that of course is the camera, which is packed to the gunwales with them.

As mine was a winter journey, the trees were bare of leaves, allowing the low-slung sun to cast its yellow rays across mile after mile of malachite green landscape. Lambing season was upon us and fat, exhausted ewes lay on their sides waiting to give birth. Smoke drifted lazily from crofter's chimneys, the noble river Towy, full to the brim with fresh mountain rain, rushed southwards. At every stop the desire to alight and hike into the hills to shoot the scene became stronger. But instead, I made mental notes at each station. Llandeilo, Llangadog, Llanwyrda, Llandovery: but four of twelve 'llans' (or parishes) in the twenty-nine stations along the line.

Eventually I reached my journey's end, where I spent a pleasant afternoon visiting the 12th century church of St Laurence. Before turning in at the local B&B, I automatically fell into my habit of reviewing the day's photographs over a glass or two of wine, only to quickly come to the realisation that, while I'd planned an entire portfolio during course of the day behind me, I hadn't taken a single shot. It is a strange admission, and yet one that not only seemed in keeping with my experience of the day, but also gave me a certain amount of professional photographer's pride, though it took me a moment to work out why.

What could be the point, I hear you ask, in being a photographer and subsequently rejoicing in not having depressed the shutter release button while in the field? To which I reply that I think there might, in fact, be three points. First, I'd temporarily broken free of the digital stranglehold of shooting first and asking questions later. Second, I'd spent a day doing something that none of us ever does enough of, and that is dreaming of a great photograph rather than actually trying to take one. Finally, I'd received a welcome reminder of why I picked up a camera in the first place. Which is to make pictorial sense of the landscape around me: something I sometimes find myself forgetting.

45

Washed out on the Jersey shore

We're taught as children that if at first we don't succeed, we should 'try, try and try again'. But there are times, as I found out on a recent assignment in Jersey, when a more reasonable course of action might be simply to give up...

I sometimes find myself seeking to explain to people who are not photographers what being a photographer is actually like. The process itself, I routinely compare with fishing, but when describing the profession, I turn to the analogy of the test match cricketer. And why not? After all, cricket is a long game in which the tides of fortune can turn on anything, from the minuscule to the monolithic. It's one of subtlety and strategy, wisdom and improvisation, technology, heritage and good manners. While the material rewards can seem small compared with the effort invested, when everything goes your way, if I may mix my metaphors, there's nothing like standing on the mountain's summit, surveying all before you with an air of quiet victory. On the other hand, when there is rain, the fixture may be cancelled without a single ball being delivered to the batsman.

Of course, we try not to think about the last bit, and I confess nothing could have been further from my mind as my plane chugged southward over the English Channel to Jersey, taking me on assignment for a luxury travel magazine that required regulation snapshots of this igneous isle, famous for dairy produce and potatoes, cut flowers and, as my research uncovered, being the only domain of Her Britannic Majesty's United Kingdom to have been occupied by Nazi Germany during the Second World War.

With the sky above a cloudless shade of cerulean and the water below an inky turquoise, my right index finger was twitching to be reunited with the shutter release button. Upon landing, I hopped into the hire car, drove west, hiked high into the cliffs at the place where the crows meet – La Corbière – and as the sun's coppery gong descended to the horizon I awaited the first ball of the innings, certain that the next few days would be easy work at the crease.

Which just goes to show how wrong we can be, because when the following day dawned it was as if Michael Fish had tempted the weather gods by informing them that there would be no hurricane. For, to mangle a phrase from Milton, all hell had broken loose. To describe how this affected my mood I turn to a modern writer and celebrity resident of Jersey, the zoologist Gerald Durrell, who once wrote that he couldn't be expected to produce deathless prose in an atmosphere of gloom. And it was under distinctly Stygian skies that I spent the rest of my time on the island, drawing a similar conclusion about my photographic undertaking. I remember how as a kid I grew weary of the annual glut of postcards sent from Jersey by octogenarian aunts that both wished I was there (an outright lie, if you ask me) and boasting of a surfeit of tropical sunshine that would give the Caribbean a run for its money. But on this day the sky was as black as your hat, leading me to tinker with the idea that if you could see neighbouring Guernsey then that was a sign that it was probably going to rain: while on the other hand, if you *couldn't*, it meant that it already *was* raining.

The life of a jobbing togger is such that you've no choice but to get on with it. And while Shakespeare might have warbled on about the 'gentle rain from heaven' in *The Merchant of Venice*, I'll lay any odds that Will of Stratford never set foot on Jersey, for had he done so, he'd have written *The Tempest* a lot sooner than he did. Here was I, with a shot-list brimful of imaginative ideas about where and when to take my photos of dairy cows, hillside arable farms and flower nurseries. And here, as my companion, was rain. Reluctantly, I did the decent thing and politely waited for the tumult to abate.

Waiting for the weather to improve is of course the bane of any photographer's life. In this case, for two reasons: first, the weather on islands in temperate maritime climates is at best unpredictable while, second, it is not in the nature of photographers to be patient for long. Now, there are two counter-positions here. The first is that there is no such thing as bad weather, and we should embrace the conditions, whatever the conditions, and seek our shot. Then there is the accusation that if you are not possessed of inordinate amounts of patience in the first place, then perhaps it might be worth considering if you are in the right job. I agree in part with both, and am often to be heard claiming over a pint at the *Dog & Duck* that patience is my middle name (a statement that is factually accurate for one of my maiden aunts), while rain is just a subtle hint from the deities that we should stop being lazy and take more interesting photographs. But, you see, I had an actual commission, which was to shoot jolly picture-postcard Jersey in an unfeasibly short time as though for a découpage chocolate box. Problem being that you don't often see a rainy chocolate box.

As I reclined on the hostelry bunk listening to *Test Match Special* on the wireless, writing up an entirely fictional account of my time on sunny Jersey, I decided to phone my editor to explain that we'd been washed out. "Got anything at all?" she enquired. I replied in the positive. "I have some telephone numbers for a couple of decent picture libraries." And with that the match was abandoned.

46

The trouble with travel photography

It should be one of those great creative windows onto the vastly diverse world we live in. And yet so often travel photography descends into a downward spiral of cliché, ending up little more than a caricature of itself.

A funny thing happened to me the other day. The editor of a swanky lifestyle magazine told me that, while he was happy to publish the piece I'd written about a recent safari in Zambia, he was slightly *unhappy* with my photos, and would prefer to research his own. Although deep down I was offended, outraged and mortally wounded, I managed to quickly talk myself into realising that people have their reasons, and there wasn't much I could do about it. I also came to grudgingly accept that from the editor's point of view it was conceivable there might possibly be something wrong with my lion photographs. Although it was probably the wrong thing to do, towards the end of the phone call I was unable to resist enquiring what that might be. To my amazement I was told: "not yellow enough." It was at this point that I started to think it was perhaps not so funny, after all.

My article has now been published along with library shots of obviously captive cats as yellow as bananas, post-processed to the point where my eyes virtually started to bleed. I've been travelling all over sub-Saharan Africa for decades and I've never seen a lion that colour before. As we all know, they're tawny, silvery-brown or occasionally a shade of burnt gold that's a wonder to behold. For the record, the official colour 'lion' (hex triplet #C19A6B) that 'represents the average colour of the fur of a lion' can best be described as walnut in hue.

The story of my imperfectly coloured lions seems to sum up one of the biggest problems facing travel photography these days, in that reality is often sacrificed on the altar of cliché. The photographer is being coerced into submitting work that will look good in print, rather than documenting what the traveller will end up seeing. And while this might seem to be simply the cost of doing business, it comes perilously close to an ethical cul-de-sac when we end up with lions that look like Aslan from the movie of *The Lion, the Witch and the Wardrobe*.

Now, I know this isn't always the fault of the photographer, because you're usually told by the commissioning editor that what is required of your photography is exactly what was seen in the travel section of last week's Sunday supplements. If what was seen in last week's Sunday supplements was, for example, an unfeasibly yellow lion, then that is your mission. Take it or leave it. This is the genre at its most derivative and commercial, and it reminds me of the alchemical symbol of the serpent Ouroboros eating its own tail. While Carl Jung interpreted this circularity as representing fertility and rebirth, when applied to travel photography, it's much easier to see it as self-cannibalism.

As a result, what we tend to see in the media is a cynical and ruthless idealisation of travel, where the recycling of clichés reaches a crescendo in which images cease to perform their function as a visual signal. Worse, travellers start to see the object of travel as merely the acquisition of their own version of these clichés as a form of proof that they've been where they say they have. This idyll is further perpetuated by an increase in illustrated travel books in countdown format exhorting us to go to various honey-trap locations before we die. While we should good-naturedly accept this as being no more sinister than typical marketing nonsense, it's worth bearing in mind that making consumers feel like idiots for not parting with their hard-won cash is a blatantly hostile tactic. And it's also worth considering that for most of us it doesn't make that much sense to plan holidays for *after* we die...

Despite being bizarrely underhand, these books on one level serve a purpose, I suppose. Which is that, similar to compilation CDs of classical music from television car adverts, they package aspirations in lowest common denominator terms. And they work. Despite my cynicism, I'm reluctantly prepared to admit that I got conned too. A few years ago, I was in an airport bookshop idly thumbing my way through one, when I caught myself thinking "that's it. I'm going to the Angkor Wat temple complex in Cambodia to photograph it for myself." I'd been gulled into rationalising that this was the one place that I should get to before karmic retaliation felled me in my tracks.

As I was waiting for a flight to Reykjavik, I had other things on my mind and forgot all about Angkor Wat until a few months later, when a chance meeting with a travel magazine editor in a pub in Oxford resulted in me homeward bound armed with a commission to go on assignment to Indochina. What sort of thing did she have in mind in terms of a shot-list? "Oh, the usual stuff,' she replied, and I have to say I sort of admired her honesty. After which, my attitude was that the entire enterprise would be what our American brethren call a slam-dunk.

But there was a niggle in the back of my mind created by the fact that after researching Angkor Wat, I started to realise that the overwhelming majority of photos were 'the usual stuff'. And yet, there was a diamond in the dirt in the form of Steve McCurry's monograph on the subject, *Sanctuary*, which is in a league of its own. The word has lately been robbed of its original meaning, but McCurry's photos are literally iconic (as in the Greek *eikōn*, or 'image').

They were also images that would never make it to today's shouting travel pages, but would gracefully find a home in photographic galleries and museums of modern art. I don't suppose avoiding the clichés of lesser mortals was high on McCurry's creative agenda when he shot Angkor Wat. But it should be on ours. That's something to really aim for. So, let's leave those yellow lions where they belong: on national flags, heraldic devices and in children's books.

47

Outdoor photography from a different time and space

The day we finally set foot the moon was one of the defining moments in the history of humankind. Recording all this on his Hasselblad film camera was Apollo 11 Commander, Neil Armstrong

A little more than half a century ago, on 20th July 1969, at 02:56:15 UTC, Commander Neil Armstrong of the *Apollo 11* space mission took his "small step for [a] man" and became the first human to set foot on the surface of the moon. A crackle of static in the audio transmission meant that the small, but all-important word 'a' was never distinctly heard back on Earth, completely upsetting the dramatic impact of the momentous second clause of the sentence, which was "one giant leap for mankind."

Nineteen minutes later, Lunar Module Pilot Edwin 'Buzz' Aldrin Jr. followed his commander onto the unknown surface of this brave new world. The 'astronaut-explorers', as they were described in a NASA press release issued a few weeks before take-off, had arrived.

Apollo 11 was, to me at least, one of the greatest things we've ever done as a species. In a thousand years' time, we'll still be writing books, not so much about the Cold War 'space race' between the United States of America and the Soviet Union, but the simple fact that this was the moment when we left earth to truly start exploring our neighbouring celestial bodies. When these books are printed, I can guarantee you there will be two photographs reproduced in every one of them. The first – perhaps the greatest outdoor photograph ever taken – is what we now call 'Earthrise', taken by *Apollo 8* astronaut William Anders on Christmas Eve 1968, showing our blue planet swaddled in a filigree of wispy cloud set against the Bible black of outer space. It was the first time we'd seen our home as a sphere, and Galen Rowell called it "the most influential environmental photograph ever taken."

The second is of an *Apollo 11* spaceman standing on the grey dust of the lunar surface, a reflection of the photographer clearly visible in his visor. The spaceman is Aldrin and the photographer Armstrong. We all know that. But what we might not readily know is that the camera is an EVA (or 'extravehicular activity') Hasselblad 500EL/M with a 60 mm lens: in some respects a bog standard 6x6 cm medium format film camera, and in others a miracle of engineering that told us, in a way that words never could, of the adventure.

Of course, this wasn't the only camera the astronauts had with them (they, in fact, had three Hasselblads – the other two being an IVA 'intravehicular' model with an 80 mm lens, and a spare left with third crew member Michael Collins in the orbiting Command Module). But, it is this particular specially-modified, silver-painted instrument that was to change radically our relationship with the known universe. At least for a while. Today, we've lost interest in our only permanent natural satellite. Only four of the twelve people to have ever walked on the moon are still alive to tell of their glorious accomplishment, while, of the earthbound population that watched those grainy live television broadcasts, more than half are dead.

When I spoke to Buzz about all this a few years ago, the great man reminded me that he wasn't the main photographer responsible for those classic lunar stills (although he did take the first exposure ever shot on the moon). His photographic role was to take geological references on a Kodak stereo camera. Armstrong was the man wielding the Hasselblad. And while Buzz was to be denied the chance to take the most famous photos ever made, it would seem that – as with Tenzing Norgay on the summit of Mount Everest in 1953 – a consoling perk of being the *second* person to achieve one of the all-time feats of exploration is that you get to be in the majority of the 'hero' shots. Not that there were many. By the time the Lunar Module had separated from the Command Module and was making its descent, the landing party had merely three fresh film magazines to their name: two colour and one black-and-white.

Although it pains me to admit it, we live in a world where there is a rapidly growing number of lunatics that deny the Lunar Landings ever happened. Most of their reasoning is so outlandish you can't help laughing. But something to have unnecessarily puzzled conspiracy theorists over the years is the presence of faint crosses on the photos taken by Armstrong. These are, in fact, fiducial markers created by the insertion of a Réseau plate (a clear piece of glass bearing crosshatches that was a common method of producing reference points on photographs in pre-digital scientific photography – 'fiducial' comes from the Latin *fiducia*, meaning 'trust'). The idea is that if the crosses are spaced evenly on the final image, then the photo is free from distortion, which is handy when it comes to calculating distances and heights. The fact that the Lunar Landing deniers would resort to using such a recherché aspect of technology to support their claims, in my book at least, only adds to the overall flimsiness of their argument. To be honest, it all seems a far cry from the wording on the plaque unveiled by Armstrong on the descent stage of the lunar module (that is still on the moon) reading: "We came in peace for all mankind."

It's only a small part of a much bigger story. But for the record, the *Apollo 11* moonwalkers left their 'EVA' Hasselblad on the moon, making it (so far as my research can uncover) the only stills camera – such as the ones once used by the likes of you and me – that is, to this day, literally 'out of this world.'

48

When photography falls foul of the law

*A regulation press photo-call in the Pyrenees descends
into a comedy of errors when a mix-up over a ski pass
headshot and passport portrait results in a farcical brush
with the law. You really can't make this stuff up...*

In moments of idleness my thoughts often stray to what a
good idea it would be to have an anthology of absurd
anecdotes about photography. You know the sort of thing:
ask fifty photographers for a sketch of their most
memorably daft experiences in pursuit of their trade, get a
cartoonist to dress it up with a few silly illustrations, slap
it between two boards and call it a book. If such a project
were to set sail, and assuming the editor curating this
florilegium approached me, I'd have a corker for the ages.
I've yearned to tell it for years, and it goes like this.

    Once upon a time, long before the days of digital
photography, smartphones and social media, I found

myself among a press contingent dispatched to Andorra. We were guests of a Japanese motorcycle manufacturer that was launching the latest incarnation of its quad bike. As it all seemed straightforward, my editor packed me off to this tiny principality with a simple brief involving little more than getting "a handful of shots and a few hundred words." Realising that no self-respecting journalist would ever go on these tedious press junkets for the product release story alone, the Japanese manufacturer of motorcycles under review had enhanced the prospect by tacking on a few days' skiing at a resort in Andorra la Vella, where we would also 'sample the region's night life'. While to those outside the world of journalism this might seem like outright bribery, to those within it's a simple matter of custom and practice.

All went well. Having executed a few rolls of transparency film on which I captured the required images of one of the presenters of *Top Gear* posing atop the new quad bike – that he was later to crash into a tree – I recorded the requisite interviews for the accompanying article and started to look forward to a spot of Pyrenean mountain photography. All of which went well, too.

In fact, it went swimmingly well, to the point that the media liaison panjandrum decided, rather unwisely, to take the entire press contingent to a bar for some *après-ski* carousing. Even that went quite well, until things got out of hand in a very British fashion, in the form of a drunken scuffle that led to one of the press toggers being led away by a brace of baffled local *policia* to the local *calabozo*. I wasn't involved in any of this because, at the time I was on stage playing Chuck Berry covers with the resident band that was missing their regular guitarist.

But I was to become implicated in what followed when the media liaison person, deducing correctly I was the least ebrious Brit in the bar, halted me in the middle of an extremely uplifting version of *Roll Over Beethoven*, before apologetically dragging me off to the police station to plead for mercy on the miscreant's behalf.

To those wondering what on earth this has to do with photography, don't leave the room just yet, because all will soon become clear. Having reached my destination, I went up to the desk sergeant and asked him in my rudimentary Spanish if we could have our friend back. Under normal circumstances, said the gendarme, with the air of a man who disliked paperwork, you would be welcome. Only you can't, because he can't identify himself. "And so," quoth the rozzer, "he stays where he is until he can." I reassured the official that I'd be, if not delighted, then moderately willing to return to the hotel to fetch his passport. "Oh, he's got his passport," came the reply. Curiouser and curiouser, thought I.

As little as I wanted to, I became more intricated and requested of the policeman a consultation with our hapless photographer. I was taken to a cell that actually had bars like in the old Wild West movies. After several attempts, I managed to convey to him that I wished to see his passport. It was the work of a moment to discover that the page where his passport photo should have been had been literally defaced by a rectangular hole the exact shape and size of said portrait. The policeman had been correct: the detainee was unable to identify himself to the satisfaction of the law due to his documentation being weirdly vandalised. I started to wonder how, if he ever got out of jail, he'd ever get back to Blighty.

Over the course of a frustrating hour I pieced together what happened. On arrival at our hotel at the ski resort, in common with all the other journalists in the press cadre, our photographer had been presented with a ski pass. In those days, as a nod to security and as a counter-forgery measure, these passes usually required both your signature and the affixation of a small photographic headshot, not entirely dissimilar to a passport photo, before they were officially laminated. "It said 'affix passport photo here'..." wailed the photographer.

I returned to the expectant desk sergeant shaking my head. "It appears," I said in my best but rickety Spanish, "that the true crime here is not one of drunkenness, but of stupidity. I can't help him. He is beyond reason. You can keep him."

To which the policeman threw me a doleful look, as if to say he'd never seen anything quite like it, and I don't suppose he ever had. And I don't suppose either that he thought for one minute that he'd ever make his way into an anthology of anecdotes about photography.

49

Bowled over by the decline
of cricket photography

*No-one could seriously argue that modern cricket
photography is a patch on how we once looked at the
sport. While today's images are crisp and excellent, the
old way of doing things seemed to say so much more.*

Something you don't see a lot of these days is cricket
photography. I'm not talking about today's neat and tidy
reportage imagery you see in newspapers and specialist
sports magazines, those superb snapshots of seemingly
impossible catches in the gulley, or the post-wallop
posturing of batsmen basking in the camera's gaze after
hoiking the ball miles over cow corner. I'm talking about
a graceful style of photography that seems to have fallen
out of the game's orbit: that of the deft snapper who, with
all the aplomb of the crafty magician's assistant, once
captured the character of a sport that in days of old
represented all that was good about how we lived our

lives. Flick back through a few dog-eared newspapers, copies of Wisden or cricketing autobiographies, and you'll see fabulous pictorial narratives of proud men of many nations united by fair play, respect for the opposition, a love of the game and friendship.

You don't have to tell me that this is to look back through a rose-tinted wide-angle lens. But, if ever there was a photographic subject in which we could indulge our fantasy of Albion and honour, then this is surely it. As a youth I would read and read again my Dad's battered clothbound biographies of Dennis Compton, Colin Cowdrey and Fred Trueman, absorbing every nuance of what it meant to represent your country.

The black-and-white plates in these books would always show glorious headshots of these idols – noble, steely-eyed and determined – sporting their country's caps, clean-shaven, donning fabulous blazers, smoking a well-earned Woodbine. Match shots were rarely included, as the telephoto technology required to take close-ups of batters or bowlers 80 yards away in 'the middle' was beyond the pocket of even the flushest of news agencies at the time. But more importantly, that wasn't how the editors of the sports pages wished to portray the symbolic nature of the game. Instead, we had full-length 'action' portraits of cricketers posed by the wicket in heroic stances, willow raised in anticipation of the long hop, often without gloves and never with helmet.

And I think that this is one of the main reasons, as good as it is, contemporary cricket photography can't quite convey the spirit of the contest between leather and willow, sinew and guile, batter and bowler. While once there were athletic men with varsity ties threaded through the belt loops of their whites, today we see gym-ripped muscle-machines in polyurethane body armour, plastered with sponsorship logos and tattoos, inoculated against the short ball by headgear that literally removes the face from the game. To lessen this anonymity and presumably also to compound the offence, we put numbers and names on the backs of fluorescent shirts. Talking of which, most national cricket authorities, it seems, consider green to be the best colour for their kit. This is a fundamental error if you ask me, not so much because it gives the fielding eleven an unfair advantage, but because it makes photographing the unfolding outfield drama a nightmare.

All this is a shame because modern cricket should be one of the great subjects for the outdoor photographer. I once knew a keen amateur whose mission it was to photograph every test match ground on the planet. From time to time we'd meet for a glass or two and he'd show me his latest additions to the portfolio: Sabina Park in Jamaica, the Gabba in Brisbane and, closer to home, the Oval. Baz was a great togger, who as a boy had learned the craft at his father's knee, who instinctively knew that cricketing imagery was less about the technicalities of the on-field play than it was about the tense narrative of the incoming batsmen awaiting their fate on the visiting players' balcony. It was more about the oldest monocled member slumped outside the Long Room in a silly blazer, full to the gills with sherry, than it was about the team's pre-match football kickabout.

Baz's photographs should have been published as a monograph and I hope one day they will. And yet I know I was but one of the lucky few that will ever see his glorious cricketing snaps. His work effortlessly conjured up my nostalgic memories of fielding in the cowslips on Christ Church Meadow, blackbirds fluting in the great oaks, the whiff of wild garlic wafting on the insect-laden breeze, a pint of ale set on the turf behind the wicket-keeper. Now and again the missile would whistle towards you, and if you were lucky, you'd cling onto it. The ball would be oxblood red with the remains of a gold embossed maker's mark on it. Not white.

Which all seems so far away from where we are now, at least on the commercial platform. And yet the modern game, in some ways so neutered and politically correct, still has the power to photographically surprise. If I live out my century, I'll never forget one magnificent image from the world of 21st century cricket. It was shot at Edgbaston in 2005 during one of the greatest Ashes series ever contested. The battle over, two men – England's Andrew Flintoff and Australia's Brett Lee – exhausted mentally and physically, both on their haunches, are captured in a moment of commiseration and despair.

The victor places his hand on the shoulder of the vanquished, the no-longer-needed willow seems to take the weight of both men. Thanks to the boundary photographer Tom Jenkins, we still have a record of that exchange of unalloyed camaraderie, a private moment on the world's stage and the essence of what it means to be a true sportsman.

50

Photography and the remembrance of things past

From the demolition of the Buddhas of Bamiyan to the destruction of Palmyra, worldwide architecture of vast historical significance is being torn apart by ideological madness. Sometimes photographs are all that is left.

I don't know if this is a rare or good thing, but I hardly ever look at my old photographs. This is probably for the same reason that I almost never read books that I wrote years ago or listen to the records I made when I was in an indie rock band. The past is so inflexible and established, while the future contains only possibility.

And yet, after another news report of further destruction of the Syrian desert city of Palmyra, in a moment of nostalgia I got out the photographs I took of that ancient metropolis ruinous and, over a glass of wine, inwardly wept for the stupidity of the aspect of humankind that rejoices in destroying its heritage.

Here in the West, while the powers that be tie themselves up into knots of political correctness over whether to call the organisation responsible ISIS or ISIL (or whatever), as one journalist put it "this beautiful flower of the desert is being desecrated." I have toyed with the idea of calling it a crime against humanity, but that label is tragically better reserved for what ISIS has done to the people of the Levant. But it is nonetheless a crime against civilisation and history. Despite the fact that the old Silk Road city has risen and fallen many times, its further destruction to repurpose hand-hewn masonry as war materiel is bad enough: and that's before we get started on the hidden agenda, which is to create headline news in the Western media calculated to demonstrate that we care more about buildings than people.

A few years ago, I spent several days wandering among Palmyra's triumphal arches and colonnades, funerary temples and its glorious Tetrapylon. I also idled away time in the Temple of Baalshamin and the Temple of Bel, the baths of Diocletian and the Valley of the Tombs. I walked among them at sunrise, during the blistering midday sun and by moonlight. I knew then that this was a special moment in my life and yet had no inkling that each of these wondrous buildings would become a chess piece on the board of a squalid game played by mad-dog militants, extremists and revolutionaries. At the time I was just a pilgrim, no more than yet another guy with a camera, trying his hardest to get some decent images of a place I instinctively recognised the importance of, but of which I understood so little.

It turns out that the photographs I brought home from Syria were to be invested with more significance than I could ever have supposed. Today they form a part – thankfully a small part – of all that's left. I know that Palmyra was already a ruin many times over, and that history is littered with the carnage of the scorched earth policies of marauding invaders, but to have to admit that we live in an age where such wantonness still exists feels like something of an insult. The immediate generations before mine fought wars to prevent atrocities like this happening again. They must be turning in their graves to think how little we learned from their sacrifice and with what shameful reluctance our politicians step in to do the right thing.

To my mind, the destruction of Palmyra ranks alongside burning of the Library of Alexandria or the looting of the Baghdad Museum. In the case of the former, two millennia ago, the precious scrolls and books are lost for eternity and our loss cannot be measured; with the latter, in part due to documentary and catalogue photography, combined with the international effort of archaeologists and forensic scientists, many of the stolen artefacts have been returned to Iraq and the museum has been officially reopened. While there is currently no way of telling what the future holds for Palmyra, as with the Buddhas of Bamiyan that were dynamited by the Taliban, we can for now only be certain that one of the great cultural landmarks of human creativity has been obliterated.

If you want to know just how important a role photographers can play in situations such as this, look no further than the pictorial legacy left to the nation by the great 20th century desert traveller Wilfred Thesiger that is housed – all five thousand images – at Oxford's Pitt rivers museum. I confess that I was once cynical about the value of Thesiger's photography. I used to think that the quality of his images of the Empty Quarter was not much better than that of the amateur enthusiast. With the passing of time I am happy to accept that his portfolios of the Arabian Sands and the Marsh Arabs have become crucial, if doleful, hymns to a past irrecoverably lost. Were it not for the sheer bloody-mindedness of this extraordinary explorer, part of our global heritage would be lost. Not only that: we wouldn't know it was lost, because so little of what the great man saw on his peregrinations had ever been seen by westerners before.

Maybe we should all become a bit more like Thesiger in our outlook on the world we live in. If his work has a subtext, it is that nothing can ever be taken for granted. Marshes will be drained; tribal people will be driven from their homelands, while ancient cultures will go the way of all flesh. Maybe he knew that the photograph has the power to ensure that while even the greatest of mankind's monuments can crumble at the hands of criminals masquerading as visionaries, their memory will, thanks to the art and technology he pioneered, remain.

Index

215

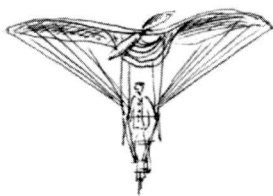

A note on the text

The 50 chapters that make up *A Camera in My Luggage* are based on my monthly column 'Inside Track', all previously published in the newsstand magazine *Outdoor Photography*. Although not presented here in the same order as they first appeared, they are nevertheless numbers 51 to 100 in an ongoing series, making the book that you have in your hands the sequel to *Travels in Search of a Photograph* that contained the first 50. As with the original volume, these pieces have been refreshed and rewritten – often substantially – to take into account the unavoidable fact that magazines and books have varying editorial demands and conventions. While fossilised anachronisms referring to anniversaries such as the Lunar Landings or the *Endurance* centenary have stayed in, I've silently removed various expressions such as 'this month' and 'last month', as well as references to the magazine itself.

Which is not to say that you shouldn't read *Outdoor Photography* every month. You should.

Acknowledgements

While writing a magazine column is necessarily a solitary business, rounding up the material and preparing it for publication in book format requires the help of others.

I am grateful to the landscape photography legend that is Charlie Waite for writing the preface. Simon Williams, art director of the *Bay* magazine designed the cover, while copy editor Nicky Watts found so many errors, howlers and infelicities in the text that it was embarrassing for both of us. Any remaining flaws are mine, not hers.

Jenny Balfour Paul drew the text decorations, and it was the late Steve Watkins who came up with the idea for the column on which this book is based.

Postscript

A Camera in My Luggage was ready to go to the printer when the photography community heard the news that our colleague Steve Watkins had died. Not only had he been my editor on *Outdoor Photography* magazine for more than a decade, but he was also a great friend. I toyed with the idea of rewriting the text where it refers to him, but decided against it because, as one of the best editors I ever worked with, he would never have put up with such sentimental nonsense. *Gorffwys mewn heddwch...*

About the author

Nick Smith is a freelance writer and photographer whose work has appeared in hundreds of magazines, books and newspapers over the past three decades. He has been editor of several monthly newsstand magazines, including *BBC Focus* and *Geographical*, during which time he has won ten journalism awards, including Magazine Editor of the Year. He is author of the acclaimed *Travels in the World of Books*, described by Alexander McCall Smith as 'a triumph' and his adventures have taken him to more than a hundred countries, as well as the North Pole and Antarctica. Educated at Balliol College, Oxford, and Olchfa Comprehensive School, Swansea, he is also a fellow of both the Royal Geographical Society in London and the Explorers Club in New York. He lives in Wales.